BIG BOOK OF ACTIVITIES

FOR KIDS

This book belongs to

THE LEARNING Journey

When we start something new, we often feel confused or overwhelmed. This is normal. As we take on new challenges, our thoughts often follow the course of those on this learning journey diagram.

From time to time, as you work through an activity, take note of your position in the learning pit. After more practice, notice how your position has changed.

YES! I CAN DO IT!

A NEW CHALLENGE

1. This is new. What do I do?
2. I don't understand.
3. I have lots of questions.
4. This is difficult.
5. I'm at the bottom of the pit! Do I quit?
6. I'm going to ask for help.
7. I need more practice.
8. I believe I can do this.
9. I'm working hard.
10. I've got it!

Two MINDSETS

The yellow ovals below contain evaluation questions like the ones in this book. The text in the rectangular boxes shows example answers. Circle the fixed-mindset responses in red and the growth-mindset responses in green.

Yes, I need to practice some more.

No, I chose a level that was very easy for me.

Did you make any mistakes?

Yes, I will ask for some help. I can't do it YET.

Yes, I gave up because I made mistakes.

Yes, I used my mistakes to help me learn.

I gave up because the feedback wasn't all good.

How did the feedback help you learn?

The feedback helped me figure out what to focus on.

The feedback gave me ideas on how to improve.

No, it looks hard, and I might make mistakes.

Can you try a harder challenge?

No, I want to practice this level some more first.

Yes, it will be harder, but I like a challenge.

3

SELF-Evaluation

Being aware of how you feel about learning and your strengths and weaknesses will help you develop a growth mindset.

Think about the times you've learned new things. It could've been at home, at school, or at a sport or craft lesson.
Then fill in the boxes below as honestly as you can.

Things I enjoy:
_____
_____
_____
_____

Things I do not enjoy:
_____
_____
_____
_____

Things I'm good at:
_____
_____
_____
_____

Things I find difficult:
_____
_____
_____
_____

Things I work hard on:
_____
_____
_____
_____

Things I avoid:
_____
_____
_____
_____

MY MINDSET Test

Regularly evaluating how you feel about learning will help you track your progress and your mindset.

Draw a face in pencil to answer each statement. Redo the test after each challenge. Do you need to change anything?

I can learn anything I want.

I am okay with making mistakes.

When something is really difficult, I don't give up.

I listen to feedback and use it to improve.

I know I must work hard to improve, even on the things I'm good at.

I enjoy lessons that are difficult and don't mind making mistakes.

I'm learning not to get upset if I get feedback that isn't positive.

I can train my brain to learn new things.

I like lessons that challenge me.

I work hard when I find the work difficult.

Key:

YES

MAYBE

NO

THE POWER OF Yet

Nobody is born able to do things such as ride a bike, count to 1000, or write a story. We learn to do these things as we grow older.

Think about your achievements so far, the things you're learning to do now, and what you'd like to learn in the future. Then use a pencil to write lists on the three jars below. You can erase and move items as you learn and master them.

Things
I can't do YET!

Things I am learning
but need to practice more!

Things
I can do!

When choosing a chili-challenge level, think about the following:

 If something is completely new, try the spicy challenge.

 If you are partway along your learning journey, try the hot challenge.

 If you feel confident, choose the mega-hot challenge.

Story Maker

> New things can feel difficult because there is so much to learn.
> It is by making mistakes that we improve.

Tell an exciting tale with this fun story maker. Roll a dice three times to find your setting, your main character, and an object to appear in your story. Then turn to page 8 to choose the challenge that's right for you, and get started!

Story Setting

| 1 | 2 | 3 | 4 | 5 | 6 |

Characters

| 1 | 2 | 3 | 4 | 5 | 6 |

Object

| 1 | 2 | 3 | 4 | 5 | 6 |

SPICY

Tell someone a story in your own words. Include the setting, main character, and object that your dice selected. Use a different voice for each character.

HOT

Write a short story. Use lots of exciting verbs to bring your characters' actions to life. (Verbs are doing words such as *charged* and *gobbled*.)

MEGA HOT

Write a detailed story. Use this story mountain diagram to help you create an exciting plot.

The Story Mountain

Dilemma:
Introduce the biggest problem that your main character will face now.

Resolution:
This is where the main character solves the dilemma.

Build up:
Show the characters in action, but don't reveal the biggest problem yet.

Ending:
Tell the readers what your characters will do next. Have they learned a lesson? Will they live happily ever after?

Opening:
Introduce your characters and the setting.

Story Maker
Evaluation

Challenge Level

Date: ....

Did you choose the right challenge level for you?

_____

Where are you on your learning journey?

What did you do well? _____

What did you find difficult? _____

What can't you do YET? _____

What have you learned from this challenge? _____

_____

Did you need to work hard to achieve your goal? Why or why not?

_____

How did you feel when you achieved your goal? _____

_____

The Secret Door

> Just because your work is not the same as someone else's, it doesn't mean it is better or worse—it's just different.

Imagine you're walking in an overgrown garden when you find a mysterious door. What's behind the door? Choose the challenge that's right for you and decide for yourself.

SPICY Draw a picture of what you imagine is behind the door. Write a sentence or two below the picture about what you've drawn.

HOT Create a mind map to plan a story that takes place behind the door. First, look at the sample mind map on page 11. Then draw the secret door in the center of your page, and create branches to record your ideas.

MEGA HOT Write a story about what happens when you open the door. If you want, you can create a mind map first (see the hot challenge above).

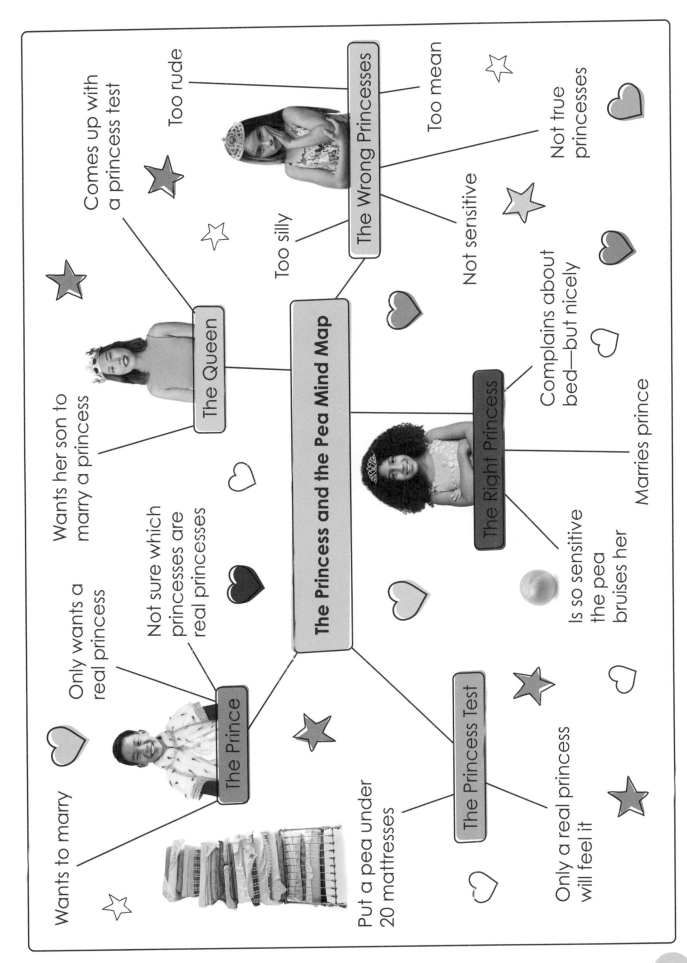

The Princess and the Pea Mind Map

The Queen
- Comes up with a princess test
  - Too rude
- Wants her son to marry a princess

The Wrong Princesses
- Too silly
- Too mean
- Not sensitive
- Not true princesses

The Prince
- Only wants a real princess
- Not sure which princesses are real princesses
- Wants to marry

The Right Princess
- Complains about bed—but nicely
- Marries prince
- Is so sensitive the pea bruises her

The Princess Test
- Put a pea under 20 mattresses
- Only a real princess will feel it

The Secret Door
Evaluation

Challenge Level

Date: ....

Did you choose the right challenge level for you?

Where are you on your learning journey?

Draw or write your thoughts and feelings about the challenge on this learning journey diagram. You could decorate the pit with emoji faces to show how you felt at different points. You could also use the stickers at the back of the book.

My Learning Journey

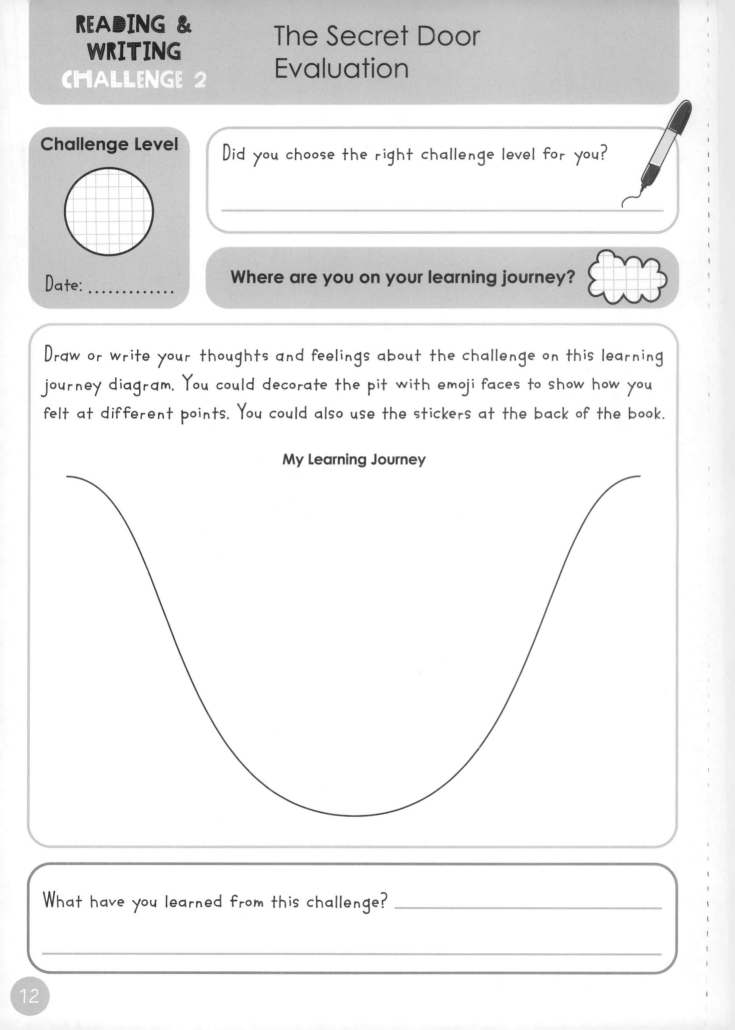

What have you learned from this challenge? _____

_____

Homophones

If you focus on understanding rather than finishing quickly, you are more likely to learn and improve.

Homophones are words that sound the same but have different meanings and spellings. **Knight** and **night** are homophones. Choose the challenge that's right for you to explore more homophones.

SPICY

Circle the correct homophone for each picture. Check in a dictionary if you are unsure.

| flower | flour | | dear | deer |

| flew | flu | | bawl | ball | | one | won |

Read the story below, and circle the correct homophone in each pair.

The 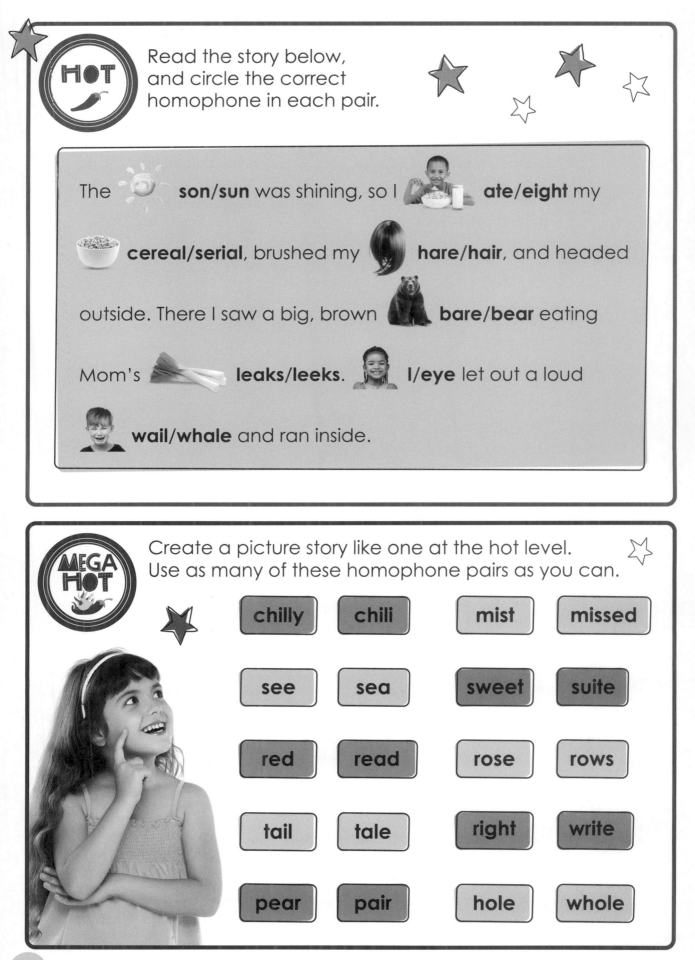 **son/sun** was shining, so I **ate/eight** my **cereal/serial**, brushed my **hare/hair**, and headed outside. There I saw a big, brown **bare/bear** eating Mom's **leaks/leeks**. **I/eye** let out a loud **wail/whale** and ran inside.

Create a picture story like one at the hot level. Use as many of these homophone pairs as you can.

chilly	chili		mist	missed
see	sea		sweet	suite
red	read		rose	rows
tail	tale		right	write
pear	pair		hole	whole

14

READING & WRITING CHALLENGE 3

Homophones Evaluation

Challenge Level

Date: ....

Did you choose the right challenge level for you? ______

Where are you on your learning journey?

What did you do well? ______

What did you find difficult? ______

What can't you do YET? ______

What have you learned from this challenge? ______

Did you challenge yourself enough? How can you tell? ______

What mistakes did you make? How did you make them right? ______

A Special Gift

Be brave and take on a hard challenge. A good activity is one that stretches you but is not impossible for you right now.

Imagine you've received a special gift. Special gifts are not always the most expensive things. Sometimes the gifts we treasure the most are important to us for a different reason. Think about what a special gift might be, and then choose the challenge that's right for you.

 Imagine someone has given you a special gift. Draw a picture of what is inside the box. Then write a sentence or two about what you have drawn.

 Imagine someone has given you a special gift. Write a thank-you letter to the person who gave it to you. Explain why the gift is so special to you.

 Write a short story about someone who receives a special gift. Why is their gift so special, and how does it help or change them?

A Special Gift Evaluation

Challenge Level

Date: ....

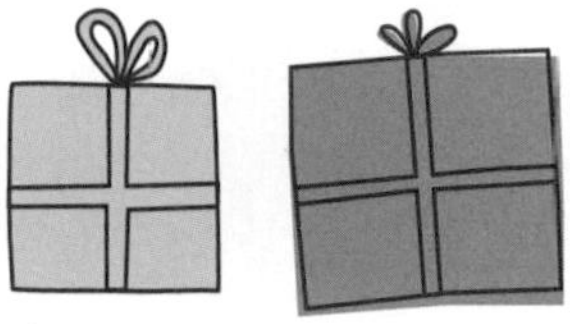

Circle how you felt when things went well.

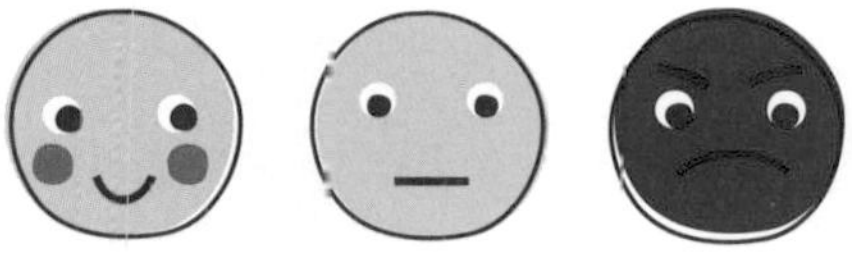

Circle how you felt when things were difficult.

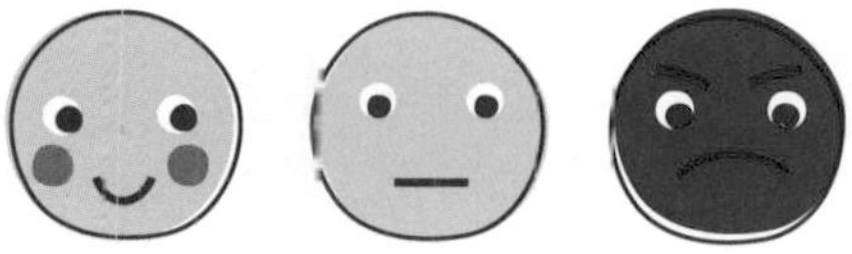

Circle how you felt when you made a mistake.

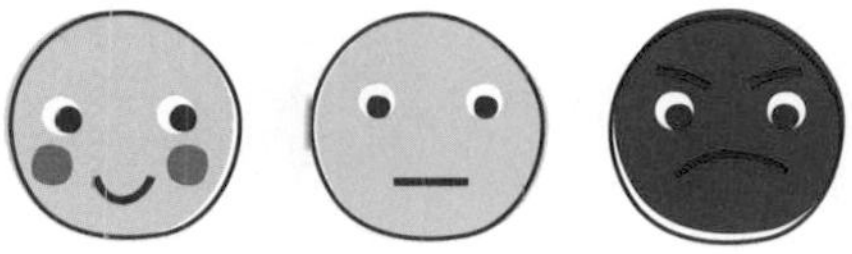

Did you try your hardest? ______________________________

What did you enjoy? ______________________________

What helped you when things were tough? ______________________________

____

What can you learn from your mistakes? ______________________________

____

What would have happened if you had given up when you made a mistake?

____

It's important to challenge yourself even if you don't succeed. If you can't complete a task, it just means you're not there YET.

The English language is full of weird and wonderful words. Choose the challenge that's right for you, and have fun!

SPICY

Zoom, buzz, boing: these words sound a lot like their meanings. Words like this are called *onomatopoeia*. Say these made-up words aloud. Do they sound like their meanings?

blurkyurky: terrible tasting
schplop: to take off and crash
foofful: nonsense
wuffiness: cute furriness
plingpling: tinkly music
hiffityhuff: a bad mood

Now make up three new words using onomatopoeia. Can your friends guess what they mean?

HOT

Use a dictionary to match these words to their meanings.

bumfuzzled	an umbrella
gobbledygook	a stomachache or queasiness
collywobbles	confused
codswallop	too complex to understand
hullabaloo	a lot of noise or fuss
bumbershoot	to be lazy or do nothing
lollygag	nonsense

Here are two of the longest place names in the world. Unless you speak Welsh or Maori, you'll probably pronounce them incorrectly, but go slowly and try your best.

Llanfairpwllgwyngyllgogerychwyrndrobwllllantysiliogogogoch

This place name is from Wales in the UK. It means: Saint Mary's Church in the hollow of the white hazel, near the rapid whirlpool in Llantysilio of the red cave.

Scotland

Wales

England

Taumatawhakatangihangakoauauotamateaturipukakapikimaungahoronukupokaiwhenuakitanatahu

This Maori place name is from New Zealand. It means: the hill where Tamatea, the man with big knees, who slid and climbed mountains and is known as the traveling land eater, played his flute to his loved one.

New Zealand

North Island

South Island

Now find and list some other long words and their meanings. What is the longest word you can find?

READING & WRITING
CHALLENGE 5

Weird and Wonderful Words Evaluation

Challenge Level

Date: ....

Did you choose the right challenge level for you?

Where are you on your learning journey?

What did you do well?

What did you find difficult?

What can't you do YET?

What have you learned from this challenge?

Did you enjoy the challenge? Why or why not?

Are you ready to try a harder challenge?

> Feedback from other people can help you improve your work. Listen and learn!

For this challenge, you will be creating and playing your own board game. Choose the chili challenge that's right for you.

Copy the unfinished **Snakes and Ladders** board on page 22. Decide where the snakes and ladders should go. Draw them lightly on your board in pencil, and then play the game. You'll need a dice and some counters.

Ask a player to write feedback on page 24. Did you put the snakes and ladders in good places? If not, erase them and put them somewhere else. Once you're happy with your board, color the lines with markers.

Complete the spicy level challenge first, and then create a set of simple instructions for **Snakes and Ladders**. You will need to include:

1 The title of the game.
2 A list of the items needed to play the game.
3 Step-by-step instructions. First, tell the players how to start the game and how to decide who goes first.
4 Next, tell them how to play the game. Explain what to do if they land on a snake or a ladder.
5 Explain how a player wins.

Ask other people to play the game using your instructions. Did they work? Did you include everything they needed? Ask a player to write feedback on page 24, and then make any changes that would improve your instructions.

100	99	98	97	96	95	94	93	92	91
81	82	83	84	85	86	87	88	89	90
80	79	78	77	76	75	74	73	82	71
61	62	63	64	65	66	67	68	69	70
60	59	58	57	56	55	54	53	52	51
41	42	43	44	45	46	47	48	49	50
40	39	38	37	36	35	34	33	32	31
21	22	23	24	25	26	27	28	29	30
20	19	18	17	16	15	14	13	12	11
1	2	3	4	5	6	7	8	9	10

In pencil, design a board game based on the hundred square on page 23. You could base your idea on **Snakes and Ladders** but use a new theme, such as:

- Pirates climbing the rigging or walking the plank
- A water park with stairs and water snakes
- A weather game with rainbows to climb and lightning to slide down.

Or you might want to invent a completely different game.

Once you've designed the board in pencil, write the instructions. Use the steps listed at the hot level. Then play your game.

Did your game and instructions work? Ask another player to write feedback on page 24, and then make any changes that would improve the game. When you're ready, color the lines with markers.

1	2	3	4	5	6	7	8	9	10
11	12	13	14	15	16	17	18	19	20
21	22	23	24	25	26	27	28	29	30
31	32	33	34	35	36	37	38	39	40
41	59	58	57	56	55	54	53	52	50
51	52	53	54	55	56	57	58	59	60
61	62	63	64	65	66	67	68	69	70
71	72	73	74	75	76	77	78	79	80
81	82	83	84	85	86	87	88	89	90
91	92	93	94	95	96	97	98	99	100

READING & WRITING CHALLENGE 6

Game On! Evaluation

Challenge Level

Date: ....

Ask another player to write feedback in the blue box.

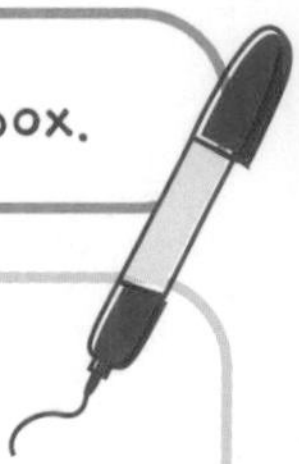

Things that work well:

____

____

Things that could be improved:

____

____

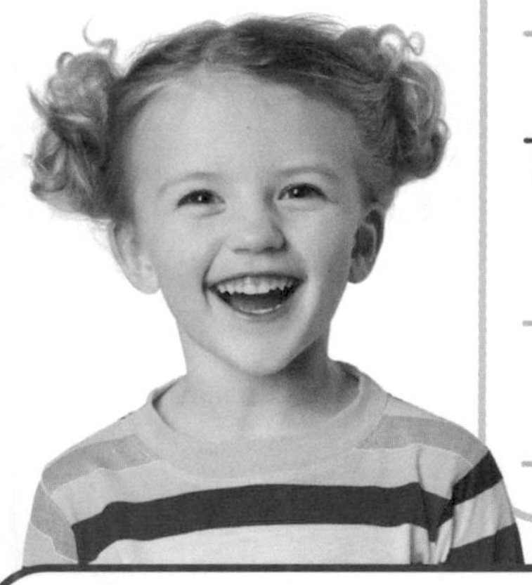

Were you able to use the feedback? ________________

How did the feedback help you? ________________

____

Could you improve further? How? ________________

____

What have you learned from this challenge? ________________

____

Vacation Island

When you're not worrying about looking clever,
you can relax and enjoy learning new things.

Look closely at the activity map below. Take note of all the fun things visitors can do on this vacation island. Then choose the challenge that's right for you.

Activity Map

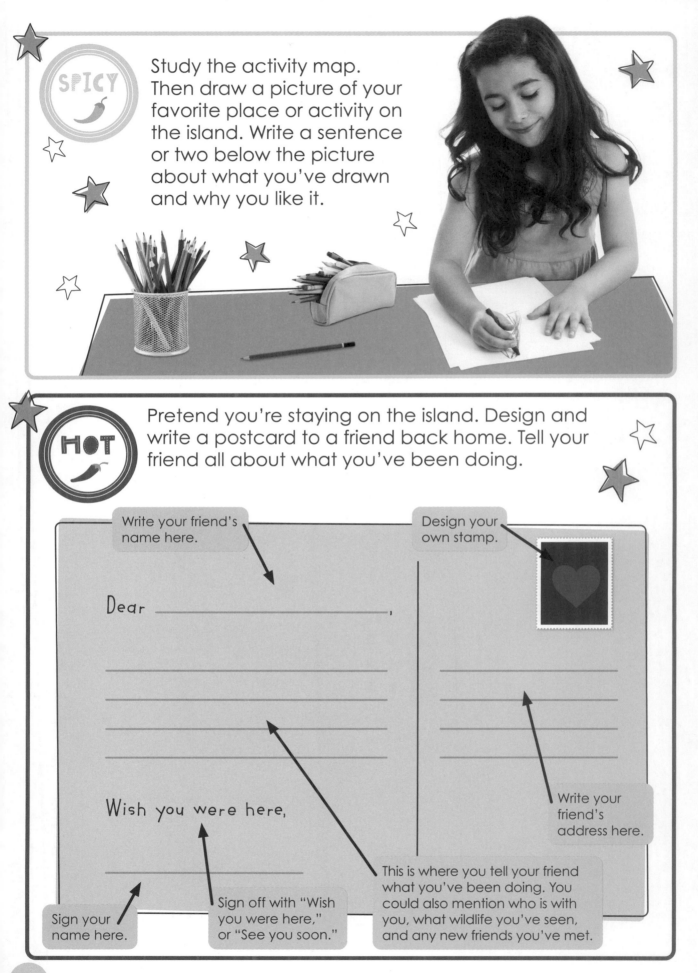

SPICY

Study the activity map. Then draw a picture of your favorite place or activity on the island. Write a sentence or two below the picture about what you've drawn and why you like it.

HOT

Pretend you're staying on the island. Design and write a postcard to a friend back home. Tell your friend all about what you've been doing.

Write your friend's name here.

Design your own stamp.

Dear _____,

_____

_____

_____

_____

Wish you were here,

_____

Write your friend's address here.

This is where you tell your friend what you've been doing. You could also mention who is with you, what wildlife you've seen, and any new friends you've met.

Sign your name here.

Sign off with "Wish you were here," or "See you soon."

Design an advertisement to persuade people to visit the island. Here's one from a rival island. It will give you ideas of things to include.

VISIT
PARADISE ISLAND

An attractive name for the island

Beautiful picture

A rhetorical question

Are you ready for a fun-filled vacation?

Paradise Island has a long, sandy beach, two Olympic-sized swimming pools, and a brand-new water park. You'll love the many exciting sports and the five restaurants serving award-winning food.

Have fun in the sun!

Enticing adjectives, or describing words

A catchy slogan

Lots of exciting information

Challenge Level

Date: ....

Did you choose the right challenge level for you?

_____

Where are you on your learning journey?

What did you do well? _____

What did you find difficult? _____

What can't you do YET? _____

What have you learned from this challenge? _____

_____

Did you think about giving up? How did you encourage yourself to keep going?

_____

What mistakes did you make? How did you make them right? _____

_____

Lava Lamp

> If you're honest about your weaknesses,
> other people will be able to help you improve.

For this challenge, you'll make your own lava lamp. Choose the challenge that's right for you before you start. Then follow the steps below.

You will need:

- a large glass or a plastic bottle
- vegetable oil
- water
- food coloring
- a fizzy Alka-Seltzer tablet

Safety note:
Conduct this experiment on a wipe-clean surface in case it spills. Adult supervision is required.

1 Half fill your bottle or glass with oil.

2 Slowly, add 1 inch (2.5 cm) of water.

3 Stir in a few drops of food coloring, and let the liquid settle.

4 Carefully, drop in half an Alka-Seltzer tablet.

5 When the movement stops, add the other half of the tablet.

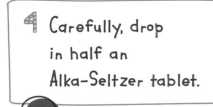

SPICY

Make a lava lamp, and then draw some of the patterns it makes.

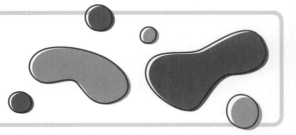

HOT

Make a lava lamp and watch it carefully.
- Which liquid rises to the top?
- Which liquid sinks to the bottom?
- What happens to the food coloring?
- What happens when you add the tablet?
- What can you find out about mixing oil and water?

MEGA HOT

Make a lava lamp and read how it works below. Then find out more about liquids, solids, and gases from books or the Internet. Create lists of different solids, liquids, and gases around your home. Which list is the longest? Why?

How It Works

The oil floats on top of the water because it is less dense (or lighter) than water. When you add the tablet, it sinks to the bottom. As it dissolves, it releases a gas called carbon dioxide. This gas is lighter than both water and oil, so it floats to the top. The gas bubbles are surrounded by colored water, which rises with the bubbles. When the air comes out of the bubbles, the water sinks back down. This happens again and again until the tablet is fully dissolved.

Lava Lamp
Evaluation

Challenge Level

Date: ....

Did you choose the right challenge level for you?

_____

Where are you on your learning journey?

What did you do well? _____

What did you find difficult? _____

What can't you do YET? _____

What have you learned from this challenge? _____

_____

What problems did you need to overcome? _____

_____

Are you still finding anything difficult? What might help? _____

_____

Balloon Power

Don't label yourself as either good or bad at science.
Focus instead on enjoying learning more about it.

For this challenge, you'll create balloon-powered movement.
Choose the level that's right for you. Then follow the steps below.

You will need:

- string
- a balloon
- scissors
- tape
- a straw

1 Tie a 10-foot (3-meter) piece of string to an anchor, such as a door handle or chair.

2 Pass the other end of the string through the straw. Then tie it tightly to a second anchor so that the string is tight, or taut.

3 Blow up the balloon. Then hold its end closed so that no air can escape.

4 Ask someone to tape the balloon to the straw while you hold the end closed.

5 Let go of the balloon. What happens?

Follow the instructions on page 32 to launch a balloon rocket. Then repeat the experiment, looking for ways to make your balloon travel faster or slower. You could test factors such as the type of string, the shape of the balloon, the amount of air in the balloon, and the length of your straw.

HOT 🌶

After making the balloon rocket, create a balloon-powered toy car. You could use an existing toy car, make one with building bricks, or make one like the one below (made with a plastic bottle, bottle-top wheels, stick axles, a straw, a balloon, and a rubber band). Next, look for ways to make your car travel faster or slower. You could test factors such as different floor surfaces or different balloons, or you could adjust your car's design.

Create the balloon rocket. Then read how it works and about Sir Isaac Newton below. Finally, use children's books or websites to find out more about Newton and his laws of motion. Make a short presentation about it.

How It Works

The elastic sides of the balloon contract, pushing out the air in one direction. This moving air creates thrust, which pushes the rocket forward in the other direction.

action

reaction

Sir Isaac Newton was an English scientist who lived in the 1600s. He explained many of the things that happen on Earth. He said that every action has a reaction that acts in the opposite direction. In our experiment, the air moving in one direction is the **action**, and the balloon moving in the other direction is the **reaction**.

Challenge Level

Date: ....

Did you choose the right challenge level for you?

_____

Where are you on your learning journey?

Draw or write your thoughts and feelings about the challenge on this learning journey diagram. You could decorate the pit with emoji faces to show how you felt at different points. You could also use the stickers at the back of the book.

My Learning Journey

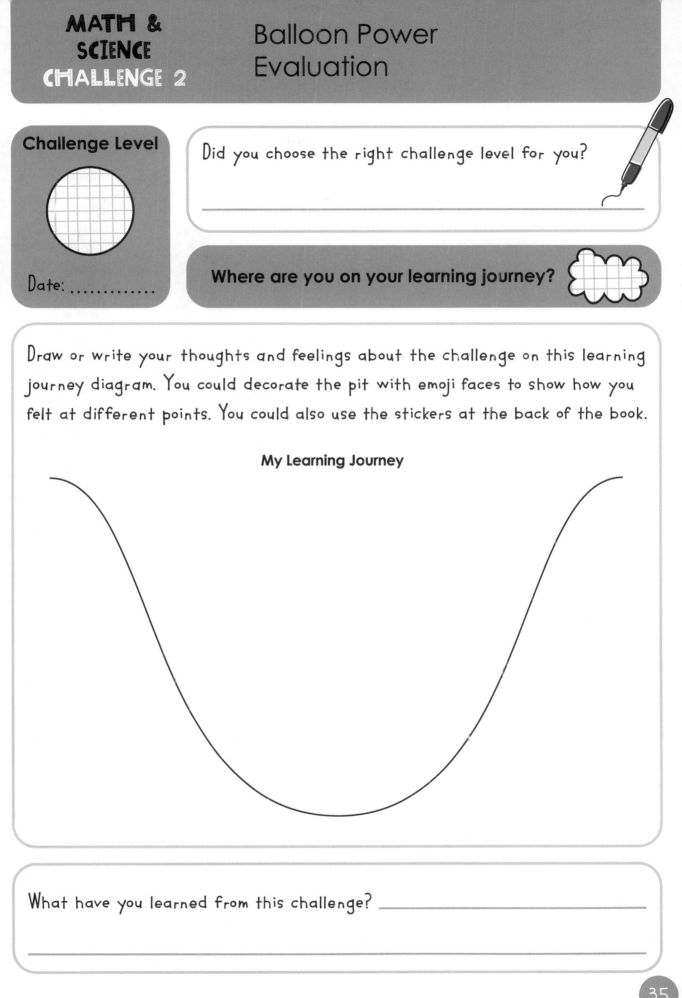

What have you learned from this challenge? _____

_____

MATH & SCIENCE CHALLENGE 3

Odds and Evens

Keep an open mind if you think you know a subject.
There may be more you can learn.

All odd numbers end in 1, 3, 5, 7, or 9.
All even numbers end in 2, 4, 6, 8, or 0.
Choose the odds and evens challenge that's right for you.

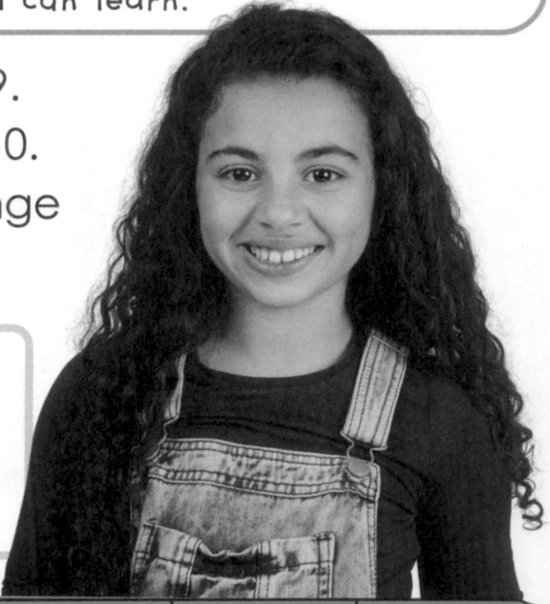

SPICY

On the number chart below, color the odd numbers red and the even numbers blue.

30	13	90	1	50	84	23
21	44	27	36	6	19	100
66	31	74	81	25	22	41
5	69	60	7	80	39	8
82	22	99	82	16	26	17

HOT

Solve the problems. Write the odd answers in red and the even answers in blue.

7 + 19 = _____

13 + 8 = _____

4 + 16 = _____

Now, use your answers to help you figure out these rules. Write either "odd" or "even" for each answer.

odd + odd = _____

odd + even = _____

even + even = _____

MEGA HOT

Make up some math problems to help you fill in this chart. Write either "odd" or "even" for each answer.

Addition	Subtraction
even + even = _____	even – even = _____
odd + odd = _____	odd – odd = _____
even + odd = _____	even – odd = _____
odd + even = _____	odd – even = _____

Multiplication
even × even = _____
odd × odd = _____
even × odd = _____
odd × even = _____

How might knowing these facts help you in math class?

_____

_____

_____

Odds and Evens Evaluation

Challenge Level

Date: ....

Circle how you felt when things went well.

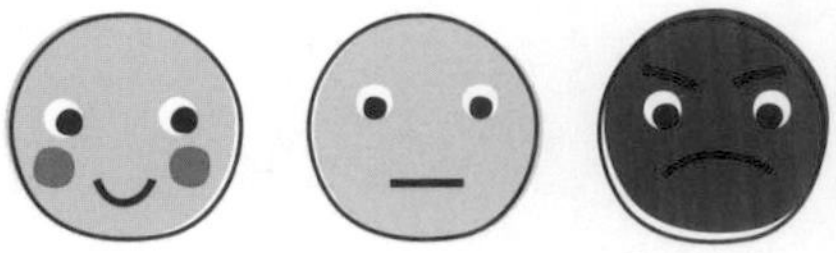

Circle how you felt when things were difficult.

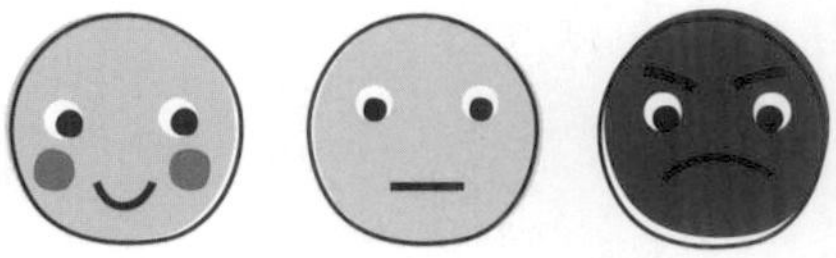

Circle how you felt when you made a mistake.

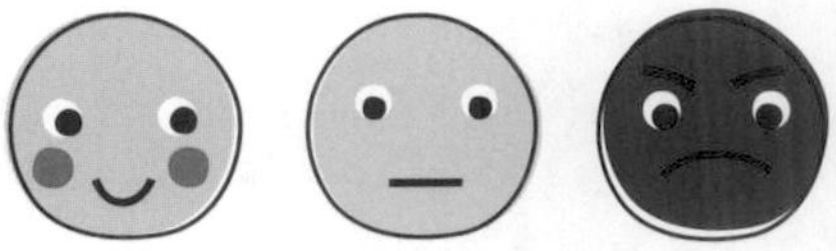

Did you try your hardest? _____

What did you enjoy? _____

What helped you when things were tough? _____

_____

What can you learn from your mistakes? _____

_____

What would have happened if you had given up when you made a mistake?

_____

Secret Messages

Remember that new things often feel too hard at first.
This is normal, and you can work past this point.

This grid is the key to a secret code. Only the grid references appear in secret messages. To find a letter's grid reference, look along the bottom of the grid to find the letter, and then move up the left side to find the number. For example, the grid reference for B is C4. Choose the challenge that's right for you and get started.

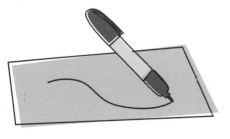

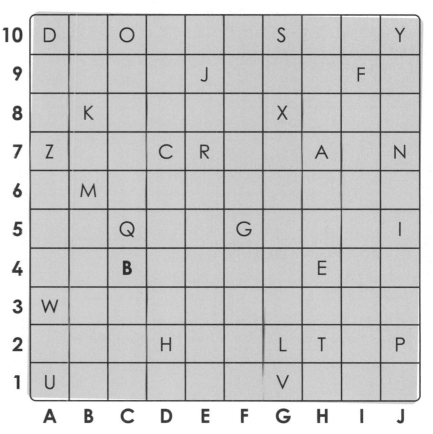

	A	B	C	D	E	F	G	H	I	J
10	D		O				S			Y
9					J				F	
8		K					X			
7	Z			C	R			A		N
6		M								
5			Q			G				I
4			B					E		
3	W									
2				H			L	T		P
1	U						V			

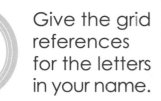

SPICY — Give the grid references for the letters in your name.

HOT — Decode the following secret message.
J10, C10, A1 G10, C10, G2, G1, H4, A10 J5, H2

MEGA HOT — Create a secret message of your own. Give it to a friend to decode. You could make your code even more difficult by reversing the order of the letters in the words.

Secret Messages Evaluation

Challenge Level

Date: ....

Did you choose the right challenge level for you?

_____

Where are you on your learning journey?

What did you do well? _____

What did you find difficult? _____

What can't you do YET? _____

What have you learned from this challenge? _____

_____

How did you overcome any mistakes? _____

_____

Did you work hard to achieve your goal? Why? _____

_____

Race Car Ramps

Don't forget that you can build your intelligence and skills through trying hard and focusing on learning.

In science experiments, we usually change one thing and measure one thing. The experiment below measures how the height of a ramp (the thing we change) effects the distance a car travels (the thing we measure). Choose the challenge on page 42 that's right for you, and then start experimenting!

You will need:

- a plank or long book to use as a ramp
- several blocks of the same size
- a toy car
- a yard stick or tape measure

1 Create a ramp that is one block high.

2 Release the car at the top of the ramp, and let it roll until it stops. Don't push!

3 Measure the distance from the bottom of the ramp to where the car stopped. Record your results in the table on the right.

4 Repeat the experiment five times, adding an extra block each time to make the ramp higher.

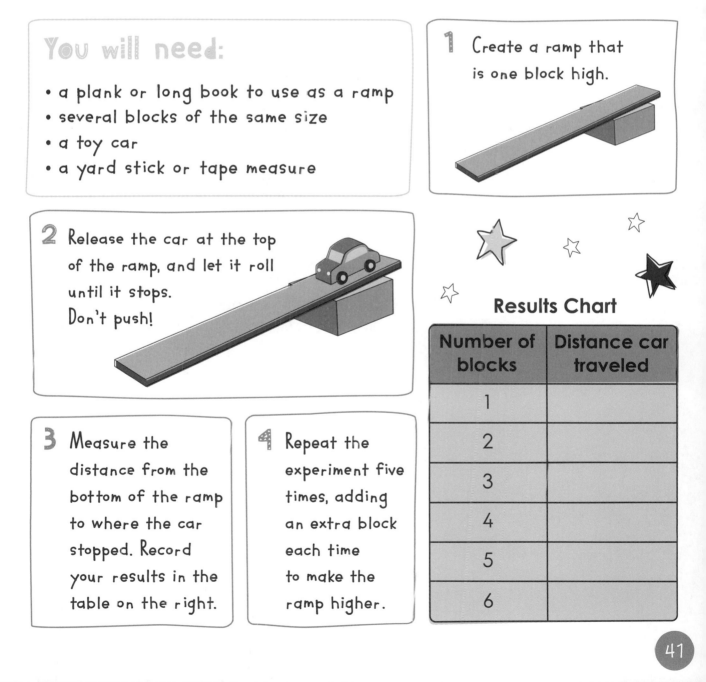

Results Chart

Number of blocks	Distance car traveled
1	
2	
3	
4	
5	
6	

SPICY

Carry out the experiment on page 41. What did you notice? How did the height of the ramp affect the distance the car traveled? Finish this conclusion:

The higher the ramp, the _____ the car traveled.

HOT

Scientists often repeat experiments several times. Carry out the experiment on page 41, and then repeat the experiment, recording your results again. Were your results similar both times? **Yes / No**

Why do you think scientists repeat experiments?

_____

_____

MEGA HOT

Carry out the experiment on page 41, and then design an experiment to test this question.

• Does a car travel the same distance on different surfaces, such as tiles and carpet?

Decide what you will keep the same and what you will change. Carry out your experiment and record the results on a chart or graph.

What did you learn? Write a conclusion here.

_____

_____

_____

42

Race Car Ramps Evaluation

Challenge Level

Date: ....

Did you choose the right challenge level for you?

_____

Where are you on your learning journey?

What did you do well? _____

What did you find difficult? _____

What can't you do YET? _____

What have you learned from this challenge? _____

_____

What parts of the activity did you do well? _____

_____

What, if anything, are you still finding difficult?

_____

Bean Journal

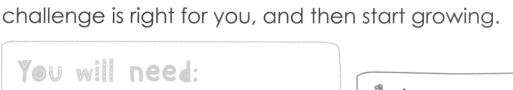

> If you focus on increasing your knowledge rather than giving perfect answers, you'll learn more and improve faster.

Each chili challenge for this activity begins with growing a bean seedling. So choose which challenge is right for you, and then start growing.

You will need:

- a jar or large drinking glass
- a paper towel
- a bean seed, such as a lima bean
- water

1 Line the jar or glass with a paper towel.

2 Tuck the bean between the glass and the paper.

3 Add a little water so that the paper towel becomes damp but not soaking wet (or your bean could go moldy).

4 Place your jar or glass in a warm, light place, such as on a windowsill.

5 Each day, check your bean. Add more water if the paper towel is drying out.

SPICY

Grow a bean plant following the steps on page 44. The time when a seed grows into a seedling, or small plant, is called germination. In a journal, draw a picture of your germinating bean seed each day. Label your drawings Day 1, Day 2, Day 3, and so on.

Label these plant parts on your pictures as they grow:

seed   **roots**   **leaf**   **stem**

Show your pictures to someone in your family and tell them what happened as your seed germinated.

HOT

First, follow the steps at the spicy level above. Then, when your bean plant is too big for the jar or glass, plant it in a plant pot or sunny garden. It will need these four things to keep growing:

light

water

gases from the air

minerals from the soil

45

Draw what your bean plant needs to grow in your plant journal. Keep a diary of your bean's progress and what you do to take care of it. For example, write down if it has rained or if you needed to water it. Figure out a way to record your plant's growth. You might want to make a graph or chart.

MEGA HOT

For this challenge you'll need to grow more than one seed. Before you start growing, design an experiment. For example, you could test that bean plants need water to grow, or that bean plants need sunlight to grow?

What do you need to change and what do you need to keep the same in your experiment? What do you need to measure? How will you show your results?

When you're happy with your plan, start the experiment and record your results in a plant journal. At the end, write a conclusion to explain what you discovered.

Challenge Level

Date: ....

Circle how you felt when things went well.

Circle how you felt when things were difficult.

Circle how you felt when you made a mistake.

Did you try your hardest? _____

What did you enjoy? _____

What helped you when things were tough? _____

_____

What can you learn from your mistakes? _____

_____

What would have happened if you had given up when you made a mistake?

_____

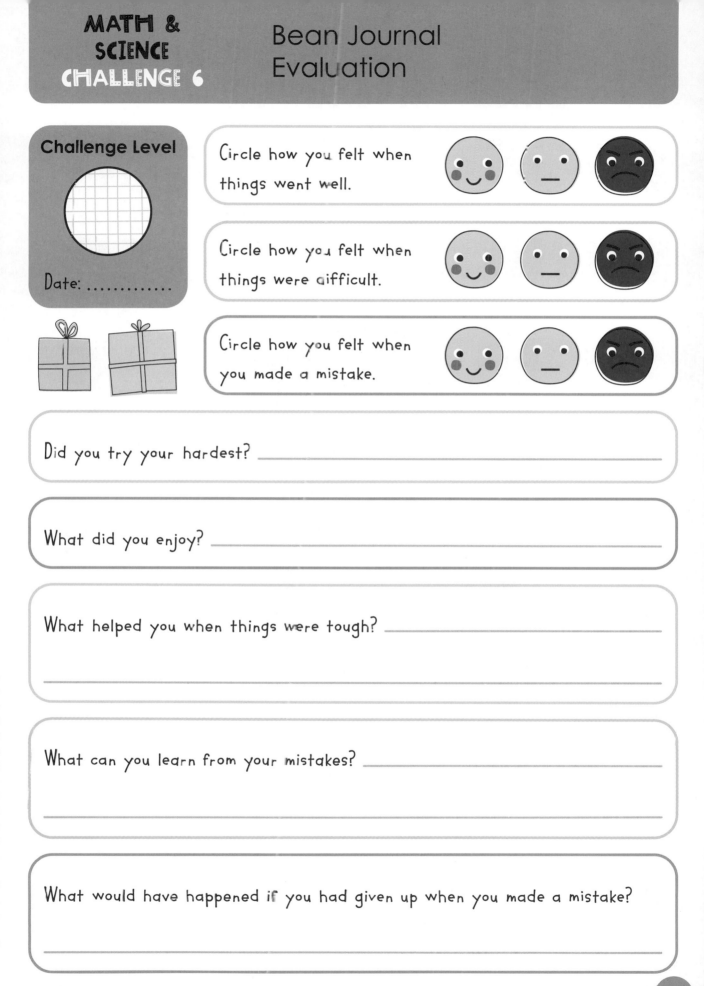

MATH & SCIENCE CHALLENGE 7

Money Spiders

No one is born a winner. If you find something easy, you still need to make an effort. If you find something hard, you can still succeed.

This challenge is to make each leg of the money spider add up to the amount you write on the spider's body. Try to write a different combination of coins on each leg. Choose your challenge level and get started.

SPICY Create a 30¢ money spider on page 49.

HOT Create a 50¢ money spider on page 49.

MEGA HOT On page 49, create a money spider of the value of your choice between $1 and $2.

MATH & SCIENCE CHALLENGE 7

Money Spiders Evaluation

Challenge Level

Date: ....

Did you choose the right challenge level for you?

Where are you on your learning journey?

Draw or write your thoughts and feelings about the challenge on this learning journey diagram. You could decorate the pit with emoji faces to show how you felt at different points. You could also use the stickers at the back of the book.

My Learning Journey

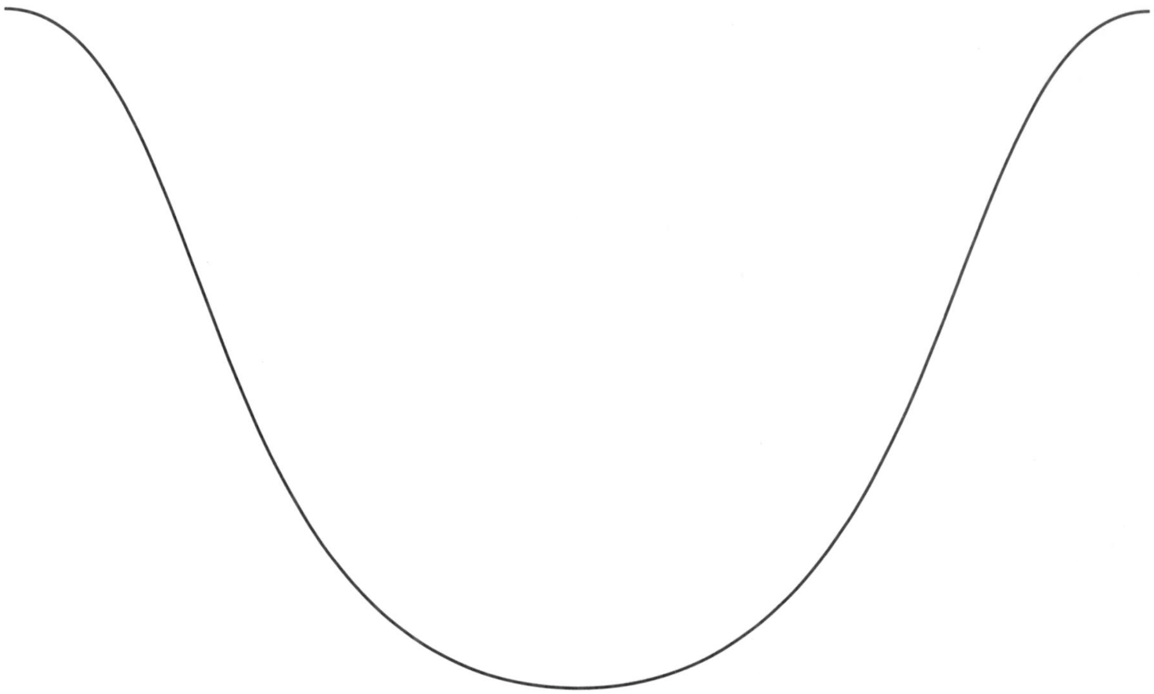

What have you learned from this challenge?

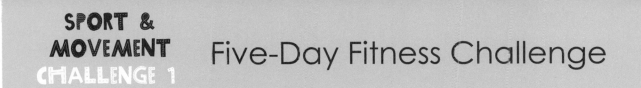

It can be hard to keep up an activity over several days or weeks. You might need to leave yourself an encouraging reminder note.

Staying fit helps keep you healthy and happy. It can even improve your schoolwork. Decide which fitness challenge is right for you. Then improve your fitness by completing one challenge each day for five days.

	SPICY	HOT	MEGA HOT
Day 1	Balance on one leg for a minute. Then try the other leg.	Practice hopping on one leg. How many hops can you do?	Invent your own hopscotch game. Play it with a friend.
Day 2	Do 10 jumping jacks.	Lie down and pedal your legs like you're on a bike for 2 minutes.	Pick up a ball without using your hands or mouth, and hold it for one minute.
Day 3	Balance a cushion on your head and walk fast. How long can you keep it on your head?	Have an egg-and-spoon race. How far can you walk without dropping the egg?	Create an obstacle course, and time yourself doing it. What's your best time?
Day 4	Practice skipping. Try to do 5 skips in a row.	Find out how many skips you can do without stopping.	Practice skipping backward. How many skips can you do?
Day 5	Throw a ball and catch it 10 times.	Throw a ball, touch your toes, and then catch the ball. Can you do it 3 times?	Throw a ball with one hand, and catch it with your other hand. How many can you do?

SPORT & MOVEMENT CHALLENGE 1

Five-Day Fitness Challenge Evaluation

Challenge Level

Date: ....

Write notes on your progress here.

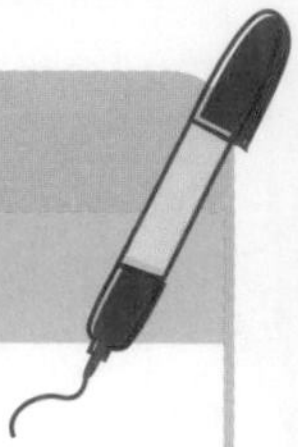

Day 1	Day 2

Day 3	Day 4	Day 5

Did you choose the right challenge level? How do you know? ____________

____

Would you do anything different next time? If so, what? ____________

____

____

What have you learned from this challenge?

____

____

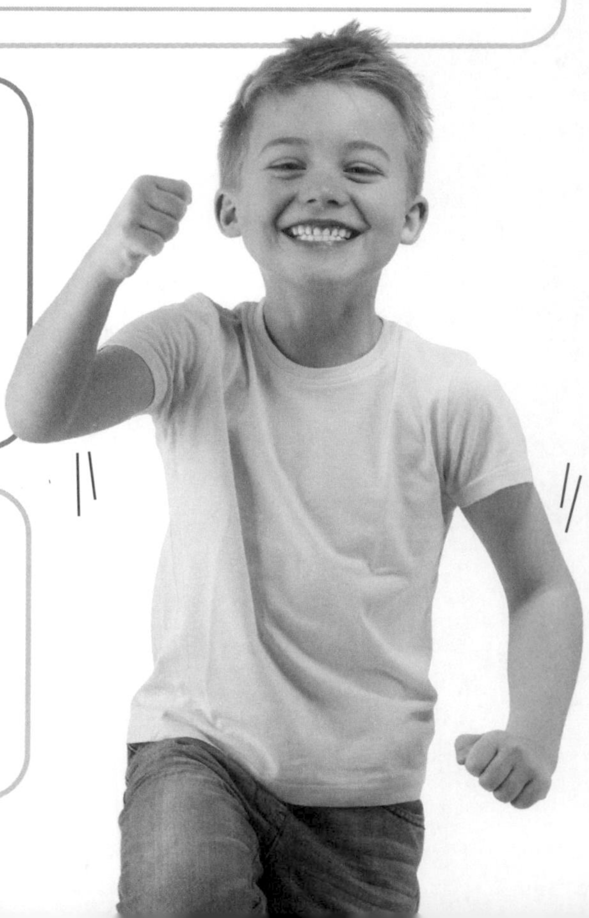

Super-Fit Superhero

Try not to compare your work with your friend's work.
Focus on making your own work better.

Superheroes exercise often and eat lots of healthy food. This gives them the energy they need to chase villains and make smart decisions. You can do this, too. Choose the superhero challenge that's right for you.

Memo to All Superheroes
Criminals are getting fitter and faster. We all need to eat well and keep fit so we can carry on catching them. Read below for some suggestions.

Superhero Health and Fitness Guide

Healthy Eating Tips	Exercise Ideas
• Eat plenty of fruit and vegetables. • Drink water and milk. • Cut down on candy and soda drinks. • Try brown bread or rice instead of white. • Try to eat more home-cooked meals than takeout. • Try new foods and eat a varied diet.	• Practice skipping. • Play lots of ball games. • Go for a walk, run, or bike ride. • Dance to your favorite music. • Go swimming. • Do jumping jacks or jump on a trampoline.

SPICY Design and draw a healthy packed lunch for a super-fit superhero.

HOT Design a 10-minute exercise plan for superheroes to do while waiting for their next mission. You could include jumping jacks, running in place, hopping, and skipping.

MEGA HOT Keep a health-and-fitness diary for a week. Each day record what you eat and drink and the exercise you do. After a week, look through the diary. Put green checks by the things that would help keep a superhero super fit. Put red crosses by the things that might not be good for a superhero. Then write some changes you could make to become a super-fit superhero.

Super-Fit Superhero Evaluation

Challenge Level

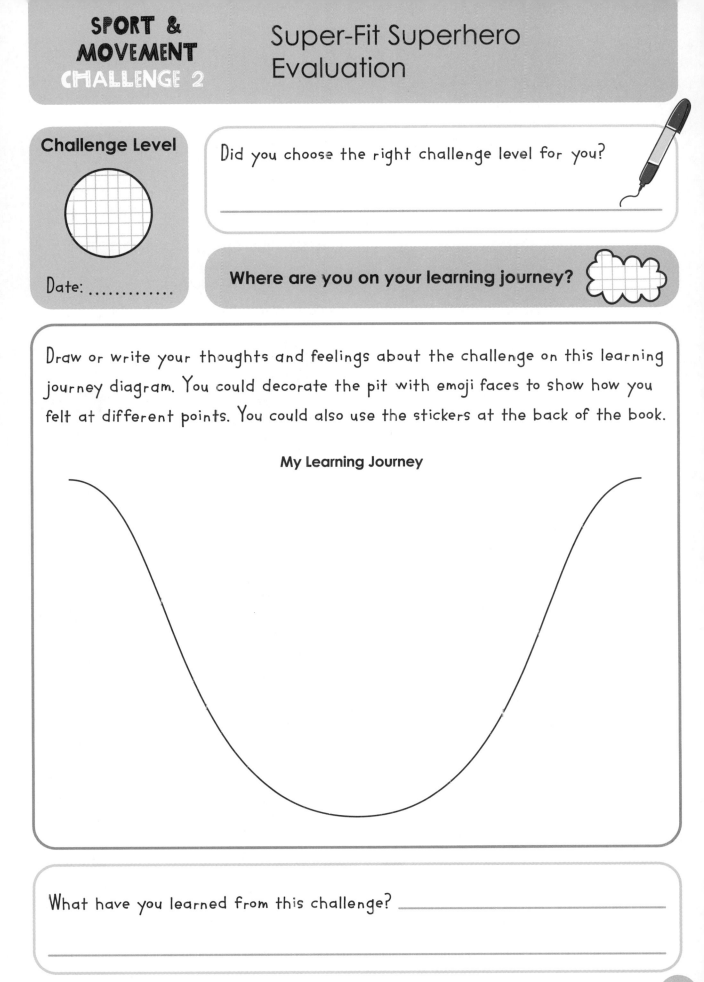

Date: ....

Did you choose the right challenge level for you?

_____

Where are you on your learning journey?

Draw or write your thoughts and feelings about the challenge on this learning journey diagram. You could decorate the pit with emoji faces to show how you felt at different points. You could also use the stickers at the back of the book.

My Learning Journey

What have you learned from this challenge? _____

_____

Soccer-Ball Juggling

> When learning a new skill, you often need to practice it many times to master it. You can't give up when you fail.

Juggling helps soccer players strengthen their ball-control skills, coordination, and balance. Read the tips below, and then choose the challenge that's right for you.

How to Juggle

1 Start by bouncing the ball with your hands to get a feel for it.

2 Then try bouncing it off the top of your thigh. Hold up your thigh so it's parallel with the ground. Bounce the ball off your thigh and catch it.

3 When you can do this easily, try to bounce it a few times before you catch it. Keep your eye on the ball.

4 Now try bouncing the ball off the top of your foot, where the laces start. Curl your toes up to aim the ball upward, not away from you.

5 Work on mastering one bounce, and then move on to attempt two or more bounces in a row.

SPICY Practice juggling with the aim of doing three toe bounces in a row with the ball touching the ground once between each bounce.

HOT Practice juggling with the aim of doing five toe bounces in a row without the ball touching the ground.

MEGA HOT Practice juggling with the aim of doing five or more bounces in a row, swapping between your foot and thigh. Try following a regular order, such as right thigh, right foot, left thigh, left foot.

SPORT & MOVEMENT
CHALLENGE 3

Soccer-Ball Juggling Evaluation

Challenge Level

Date: ....

Practice record

Day 1	Day 2	Day 3	Day 4	Day 5

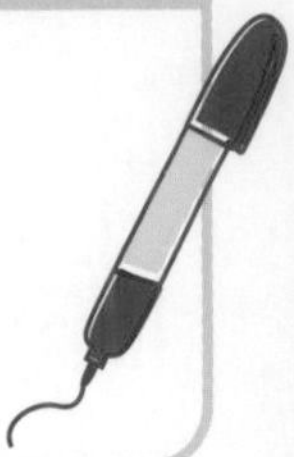

What did you do well? ____________________

What did you find difficult? ____________________

What can't you do YET? ____________________

What have you learned from this challenge? ____________________

____

Were your last attempts better than your first attempt? Why?

____

Would even more practice help you? Why? ____________________

____

Pick-Up Challenge

> The best way to improve your motor skills (or movement skills) is through practice. If you don't give up, you'll get better and better.

The ability to make the small, precise movements needed for writing is known as fine motor control. In this activity, you'll use tweezers or chopsticks to build your fine motor skills. (Use tweezers if you can already use chopsticks well.)

How to Hold Chopsticks

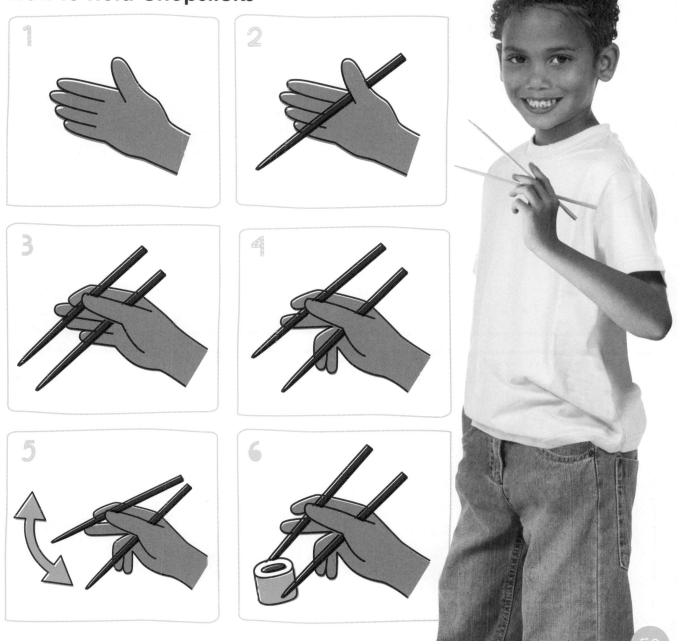

SPICY

If you don't have any tweezers, you can make some. You'll need chopsticks, some paper, and a rubber band.

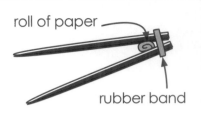
roll of paper
rubber band

Find two bowls. Fill one of the bowls with cotton balls. Your challenge is to move all the balls, one at a time, into the other bowl using your tweezers or chopsticks. Time how long it takes you. Then keep practicing to beat your fastest time.

HOT

Fill a bowl with buttons and small items from around your home. Place an empty bowl beside it. Your challenge is to move as many items to the other bowl as you can in two minutes. Use either tweezers, homemade tweezers (see above), or chopsticks.

How much treasure can you collect in two minutes? Keep practicing to beat your highest score.

MEGA HOT

For this challenge, follow the instructions for the hot level, but sort the objects into piles according to color, shape, or some other criteria as you go. If you make a mistake, correct it before continuing.

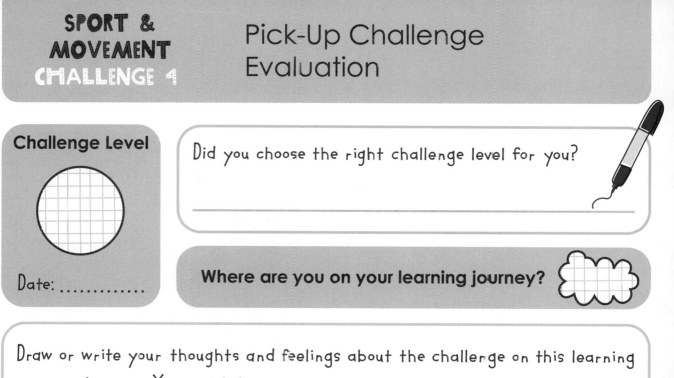

Challenge Level

Date: ....

Did you choose the right challenge level for you?

Where are you on your learning journey?

Draw or write your thoughts and feelings about the challenge on this learning journey diagram. You could decorate the pit with emoji faces to show how you felt at different points. You could also use the stickers at the back of the book.

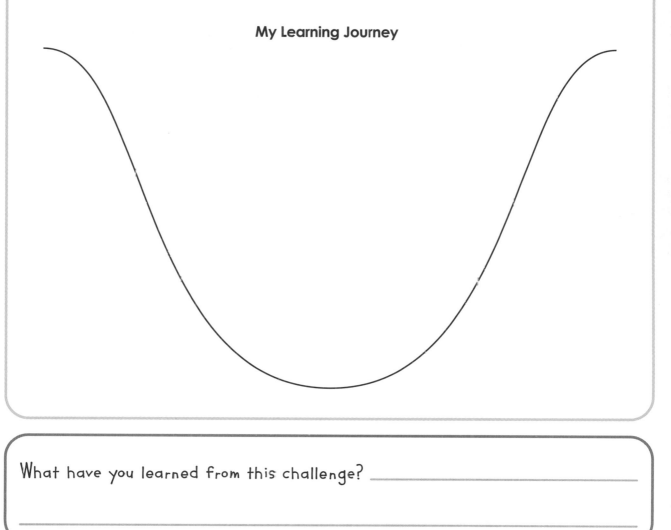

My Learning Journey

What have you learned from this challenge? _____

That's Magic!

Learning a new action such as a magic trick can be awkward and difficult at first, but the more you practice, the easier it gets.

Magicians practice their tricks over and over again. Their movements must look smooth and simple to stop people guessing how the magic works. Choose the magic-trick challenge that's right for you, and start practicing.

SPICY

1 Before you start your trick, separate a pack of cards into black and red. Put the cards of one color on top of the other to make one pile.

2 Fan out the top few cards and ask a friend to pick one of those cards and memorize it.

3 Then fan out the bottom few cards and ask your friend to slip their card into the fan.

4 Split the pack of cards somewhere near the middle and place the bottom half on top to "shuffle" the cards.

5 Look through the pack. Your friend's card will the one that's a different color to the cards around it.

6 Reveal the card.

HOT

1 Make a fan with the cards and take note of the top card in your pack. Don't make it obvious that you've seen it. Pretend you're just glancing at all the cards.
2 Hand the cards to a friend, and ask them to pick a card.
3 Tell them to memorize it and then place it face down on the top of the pack.
4 Cut the pack of cards in half, and place the bottom half onto the top.
5 Look through your cards until you spot the original top card you saw at the beginning of the trick.
6 Your friend's card will be the one above it.

MEGA HOT

1 Count out nine cards.
2 Ask a friend to pick a card, memorize it, and return it to the pile of nine cards without showing you.
3 Deal the nine cards into three piles, one at a time. Lay down the piles in a row, face up.
4 Ask your friend to point to the pile their card is in (not the card, just the pile).
5 Stack the piles so that the pile with your friend's card is in the middle.
6 Repeat steps 3, 4, and 5.
7 Hold the cards face up. Count down to the fifth card from the top. This should be your friend's card.

Can you figure out how this trick works?

Challenge Level

Date: ....

Did you choose the right challenge level for you?

_____

Where are you on your learning journey?

What did you do well? _____

What did you find difficult? _____

What can't you do YET? _____

What have you learned from this challenge? _____

_____

Did practice help you improve? How? _____

_____

What did you do when you made a mistake? Did it help? _____

_____

64

Bucket Ball

Repeating an action builds muscle memory. This is when your body learns to do the action more accurately and easily.

This activity involves throwing balls. Throwing uses your whole body and helps build balance and coordination skills. Choose the challenge that's right for you.

SPICY

Lay down a jump rope to make a throwing line. Then place a bucket about 6 feet (2 meters) in front of the line.

Stand behind the line and throw a tennis ball toward the bucket using an underhand throw. If the ball lands in the bucket, you score a goal. How many goals can you score with 10 throws? Write down your results, and keep practicing to improve your score.

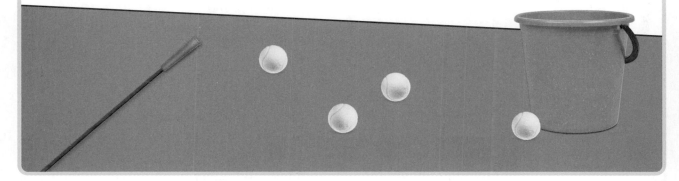

How to Throw Underhand

 **HOT**

Follow the instructions for the spicy challenge, but instead of throwing underhand, throw overhand. It is harder to throw accurately using an overhand throw, but once you've learned how to do it, you'll be able to make the ball travel farther.

How to Throw Overhand

 **MEGA HOT**

Lay down a jump rope to make a throwing line. Then set a variety of buckets, plastic plant pots, and other containers at different distances from the line.

Decide on a point system. Mark each container with the points you will score if the ball lands inside it. The containers farthest from the throwing line should be worth more points.

Stand behind the throwing line and throw a tennis ball toward a container. How many points can you score in 10 throws? Write down your results, and keep practicing to improve your score.

Bucket Ball
Evaluation

Challenge Level

Date: ....

Did you choose the right challenge level for you?

_____

Where are you on your learning journey?

Draw or write your thoughts and feelings about the challenge on this learning journey diagram. You could decorate the pit with emoji faces to show how you felt at different points. You could also use the stickers at the back of the book.

My Learning Journey

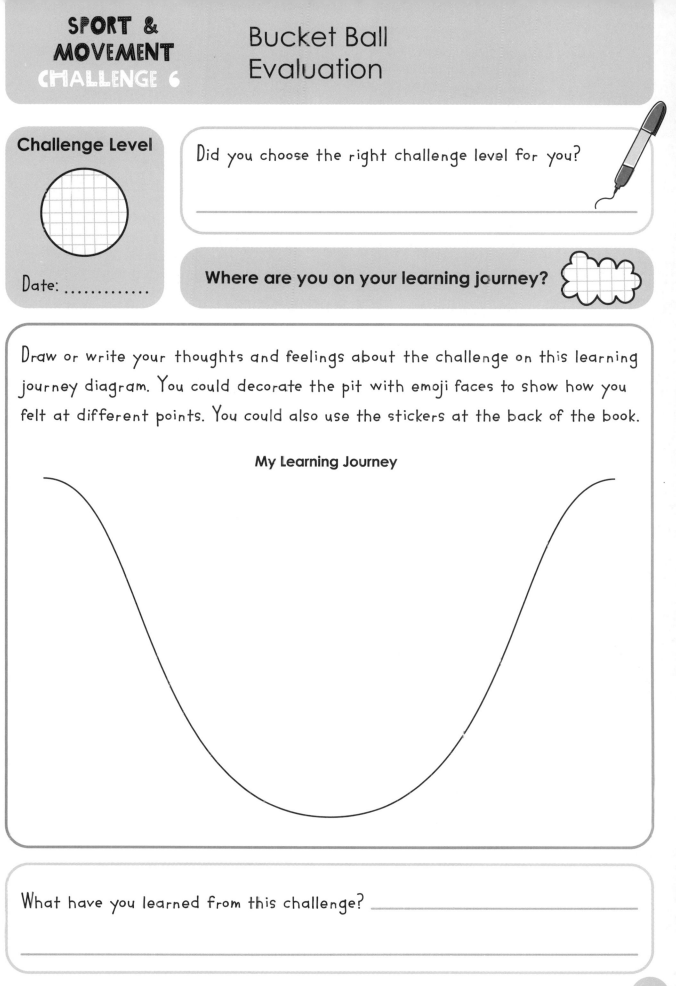

What have you learned from this challenge? _____

_____

Balloon Tennis

If, after a lot of practice, you start getting worse at something, you might be too tired. Don't give up—just take a break and try again later.

For this activity, you need a balloon and one or two tennis rackets. If you don't have tennis rackets, you could use another type of racket or make your own using plastic plates taped to rulers or sticks. Choose the challenge that's right for you and get started.

Hit the balloon into the air with your racket and then catch it on your racket.

How many times can you do this in a row without the balloon touching the ground? Set yourself a target that is challenging but not impossible, such as 10 hits. Then keep practicing until you achieve your goal.

HOT

Ask a friend to play a game of balloon tennis. Mark out a play area and add a "net" by laying a jump rope across the center of your court. Each player starts with 10 points. If the ball lands on the ground, the player in that half of the court loses a point. Keep playing until someone reaches zero.

Play again each day for five days. Take notes to record how you improve over this time.

Play the game of balloon tennis described at the hot level, but make it harder. You could play with two balloons at once or play sitting down. If you play the sitting down version, you'll need to be accurate with your returns so your partner can reach them. Work together to keep the balloon in the air for as long as possible.

Balloon Tennis Evaluation

Challenge Level

Date: ....

Circle how you felt when things went well.

Circle how you felt when things were difficult.

Circle how you felt when you made a mistake.

Did you try your hardest? _____

What did you enjoy? _____

What helped you when things were tough? _____
_____

What can you learn from your mistakes? _____
_____

What would have happened if you had given up when you made a mistake?
_____

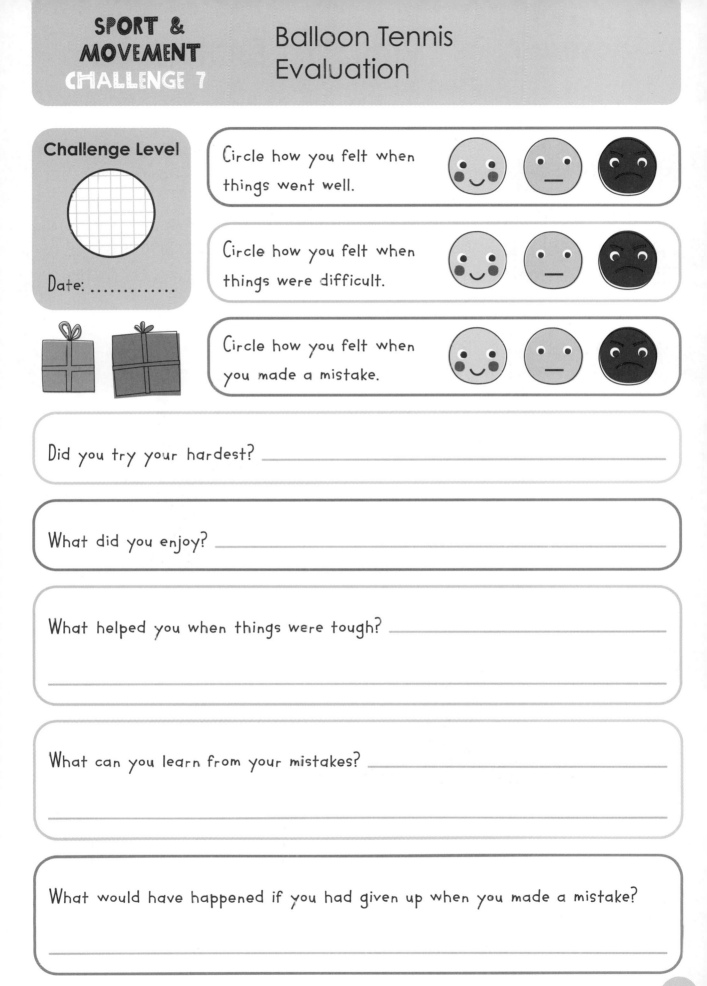

Ribbon Dancing

> To learn a new skill, you need to set yourself challenging goals, practice regularly, and work hard to learn and improve.

Ribbon dance began in ancient China. Nowadays, it is performed in rhythmic gymnastics, an Olympic sport. Dancers create patterns using a ribbon attached to a stick.

Make your ribbon by attaching about 6 feet (2 meters) of ribbon to a dowel or stick. If you don't have any ribbon, you could make some from crepe paper. Then choose the challenge that's right for you and get dancing.

SPICY

Pick up your ribbon, play some music, and dance!

Can you make the ribbon move in time to the music? Try dancing to slow and fast pieces. Change the speed of your movements to match the music.

HOT

Practice using the ribbon by twirling it about as you dance to a piece of music. Then try to make the ribbon shapes shown below. How many can you do?

Try again every day for five days. Which ones are the hardest? Spend more time on those ones. Do they get easier with practice?

semicircle	to and fro	ripples	surf
circles	zigzags	star	lots of loops
infinity sign	upward swirl	curl	wild wiggles

MEGA HOT

Follow the hot-level steps. Then choose a piece of music and create a ribbon dance to accompany it. Record your sequence of moves by drawing the ribbon shapes in order. Then practice your dance in time to the music.

Perform your dance to a friend or a family member, and ask them to give you feedback. Take their suggestions if you agree with them. Then perform the dance again for other people.

Ribbon Dancing Evaluation

Challenge Level

Date: ....

Did you choose the right challenge level for you?

_____

Where are you on your learning journey?

Draw or write your thoughts and feelings about the challenge on this learning journey diagram. You could decorate the pit with emoji faces to show how you felt at different points. You could also use the stickers at the back of the book.

My Learning Journey

What have you learned from this challenge? _____

_____

Create Calligrams

We all have different strengths and weaknesses. Everybody has something they must work hard at to achieve.

A calligram is a word or piece of text that forms an image. The image shows us what the text says. Take a look at these examples, and then choose the challenge that's right for you.

Create a calligram for three of these words.

hot	cold
huge	tiny
curly	sharp
spotted	wiggly

HOT

Copy one of these paragraphs, changing all the **bold** words into calligrams.

The **tall**, **wide**, and very **hairy** monster was **scary**. I screamed when it **jumped** out from behind a **tree**.

A **spotted** dog jumped into a **muddy** puddle and **splashed** my **checked** coat. What a **mess**!

The **hot** sun made the **raindrops sparkle**. We saw a colorful **rainbow** in the clear **blue** sky.

MEGA HOT

Create a picture from a collection of themed words or a piece of writing. Here are some examples.

ART & CREATIVITY CHALLENGE 1

Create Calligrams Evaluation

Challenge Level

Date: ....

Did you choose the right challenge level for you?

Where are you on your learning journey?

What did you do well?

What did you find difficult?

What can't you do YET?

What have you learned from this challenge?

Could you challenge yourself even more? If so, how?

What parts of this challenge might get better with further practice?

Self-Portrait

Listening to feedback from others and acting on advice can help you improve your work.

In this challenge, you'll create two self-portraits, using feedback to create a better portrait the second time. Choose the challenge that's right for you and start drawing.

SPICY

Use a mirror and a pencil to draw a picture of your head and shoulders. Show as much detail as you can. Next, ask an adult to write some feedback in the orange box on page 79. Read and discuss their comments. Then draw another portrait, keeping the feedback in mind.

HOT

Use a mirror and a pencil to draw a picture of your head and shoulders. Show as much detail as you can. Next, ask an adult to write some feedback in the orange box on page 79. Read their comments and the portrait tips below. Finally, draw another portrait, keeping the feedback and the tips in mind.

1 Draw an oval that is wider at the top than the bottom.

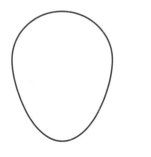

2 The eyes go halfway between the top and bottom.

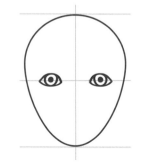

3 Add eyelashes and eyebrows.

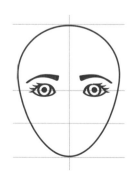

4 Draw the nose halfway between the eyes and chin.

5 Draw ears reaching from the eyes to the nose.

6 The mouth goes halfway between the nose and chin.

7 Add a neck and shoulders.

8 Add hair above and below the oval outline.

9 Add freckles, glasses, or any other features.

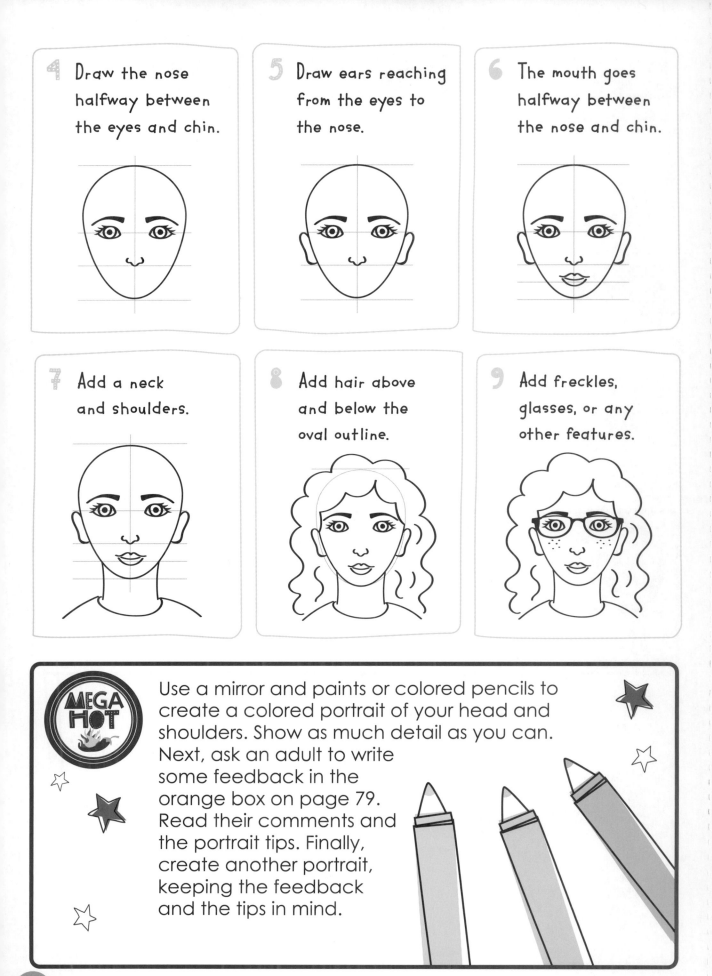

MEGA HOT

Use a mirror and paints or colored pencils to create a colored portrait of your head and shoulders. Show as much detail as you can. Next, ask an adult to write some feedback in the orange box on page 79. Read their comments and the portrait tips. Finally, create another portrait, keeping the feedback and the tips in mind.

Self-Portrait Evaluation

Challenge Level

Date: ....

Ask an adult to give you feedback on your work below.

Things that look good:

_____

_____

Things that could be improved:

_____

_____

Try again, using the feedback. Then answer the questions below.

Was your second attempt better than the first? Why? _____

_____

Could you improve further? How? _____

_____

What have you learned from this challenge? _____

_____

79

Bubble Letters

To learn some things, you have to practice them many times. After a while, they become easier.

Bubble letters look great on school projects. Read the five steps that show you how to create basic bubble letters. Then choose the challenge that's right for you.

1   Draw a simple letter shape in light pencil.

2   Draw a fat, curly outline around the letter shape. Then carefully erase the simple letters you drew in step 1.

3   Add an oval reflection on the top left of each letter.

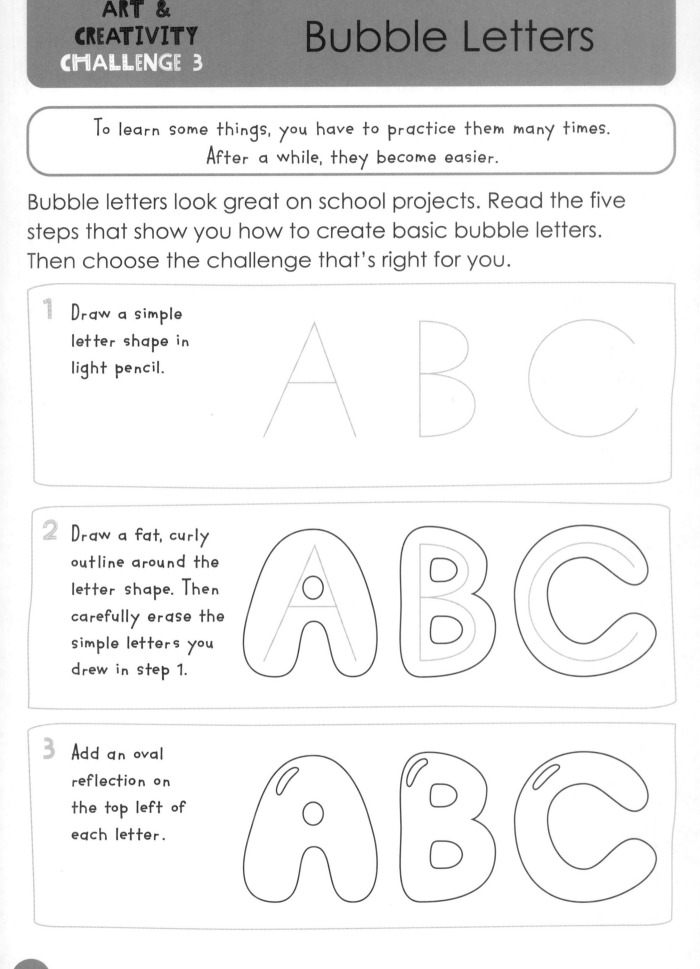

4 Add a shadow line to the right of the letter. It should be a little lower than the letter itself.

5 Color the letter. Make the shadow the same color but a bit darker.

SPICY — Practice drawing your name in bubble letters.

HOT — Practice drawing your name in multicolored bubble letters like this.

AUBREY

MEGA HOT — Write a bubble message. Use as many letters in the alphabet as you can. Use multicolored letters if you want.

Challenge Level

Date: ....

Did you choose the right challenge level for you?

Where are you on your learning journey?

Draw or write your thoughts and feelings about the challenge on this learning journey diagram. You could decorate the pit with emoji faces to show how you felt at different points. You could also use the stickers at the back of the book.

My Learning Journey

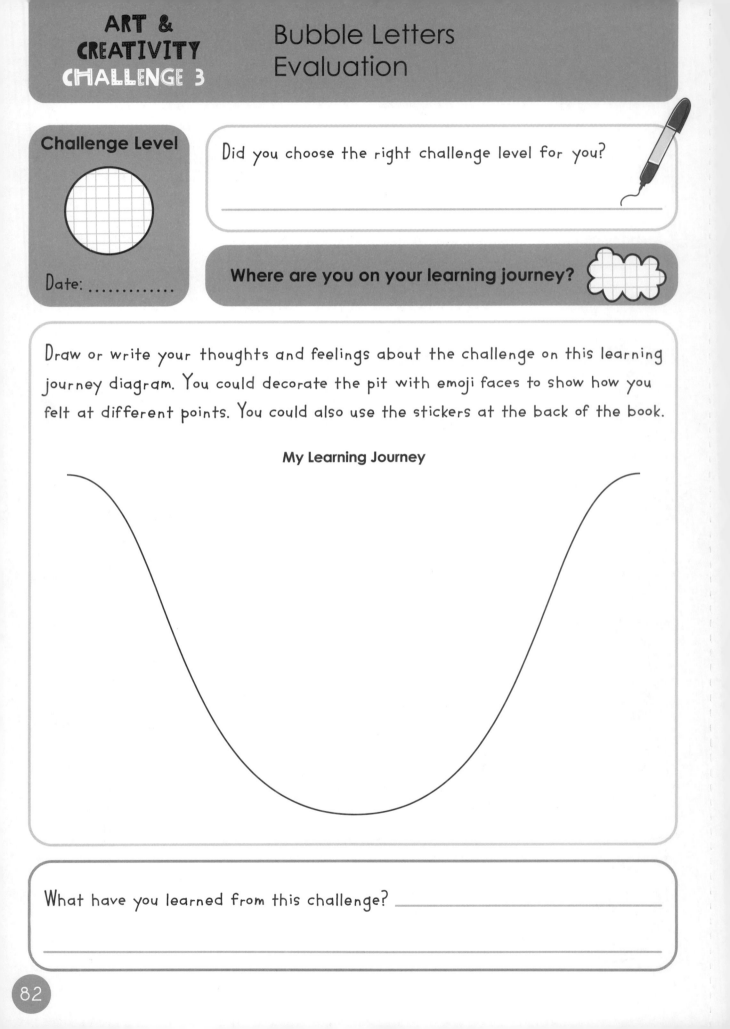

What have you learned from this challenge? _____

_____

Shape Pictures

If someone offers you advice, think seriously about their comments, and then decide if the advice is right for you.

For this activity, you'll be creating art using shapes or shaped objects. First, choose the challenge that's right for you.

SPICY

Carefully trace and cut out the tangram shapes below. Combine the shapes to make the pictures shown in the green box on page 84. Then create a picture of your own. Take photos of your pictures, and challenge someone else to make them with the pieces.

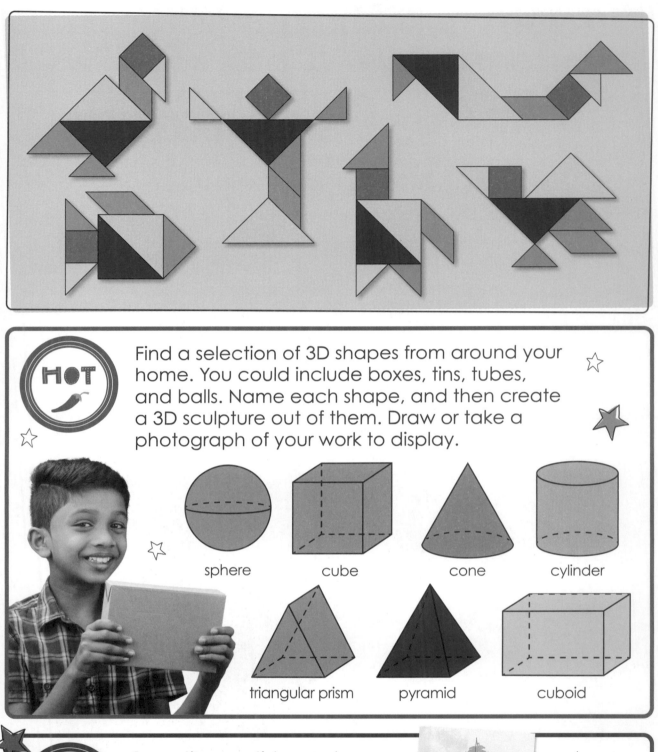

HOT

Find a selection of 3D shapes from around your home. You could include boxes, tins, tubes, and balls. Name each shape, and then create a 3D sculpture out of them. Draw or take a photograph of your work to display.

sphere   cube   cone   cylinder

triangular prism   pyramid   cuboid

MEGA HOT

Sometimes artists use shapes to create portraits. Instead of showing an exact likeness, the pictures give viewers a sense of the person's personality. Create a portrait of yourself or someone you know using shapes.

Shape Pictures Evaluation

Challenge Level

Date: ....

Did you choose the right challenge level for you?

_____

Where are you on your learning journey?

What did you do well? _____

What did you find difficult? _____

What can't you do YET? _____

What have you learned from this challenge? _____

_____

What problems did you have? How did you overcome them? _____

_____

How did you feel when you achieved your goal? _____

_____

Pointillism

> Doing well in art is not just about talent. You can learn lots of skills that will transform your work if you practice them.

In 1888, French artist Georges Seurat painted this picture using nothing but dots. He realized that when lots of tiny dots are painted close together, the eye blends them to see solid color. This style of art is called pointillism.

How to Paint Using Pointillism

You will need:

- white paper or cardboard
- a pencil
- colored markers or paint and cotton swabs

1 Draw a simple outline in pencil.

2 Fill in each section with colored dots.

SPICY
Create a simple picture of a flower or a rainbow using pointillism.

HOT
Draw a simple outline and then use pointillism to add shading. Remember, the closer the dots are together, the darker the shade. The further apart the dots, the lighter the shade. You can also blend two colors.

MEGA HOT
Use pointillism to create a landscape picture in the style of Georges Seurat.

ART & CREATIVITY CHALLENGE 5

Pointillism Evaluation

Challenge Level

Date: ....

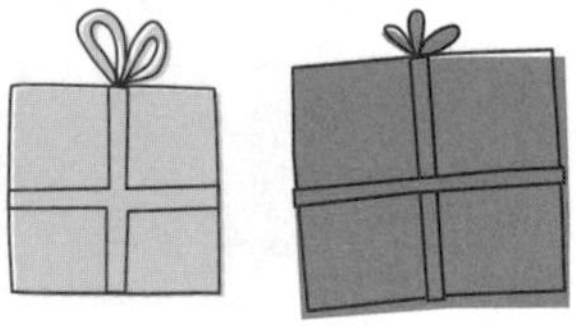

Circle how you felt when things went well.

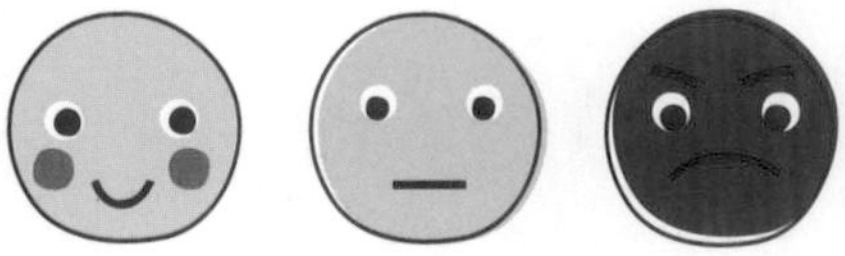

Circle how you felt when things were difficult.

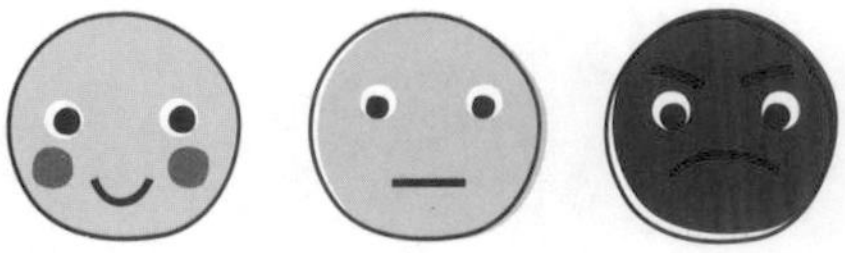

Circle how you felt when you made a mistake.

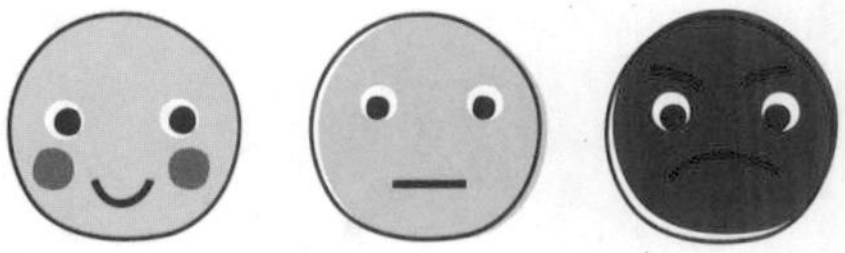

Did you try your hardest? ____________________

What did you enjoy? ____________________

What helped you when things were tough? ____________________

____

What can you learn from your mistakes? ____________________

____

What would have happened if you had given up when you made a mistake?

____

Good designers both learn from others and create their own style.
It is not one or the other, but both.

For this challenge, you'll design your own sneakers. Choose the challenge that's right for you, and start designing.

Design 1

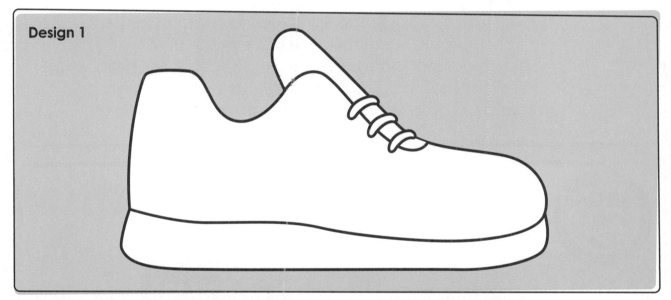

Design 2

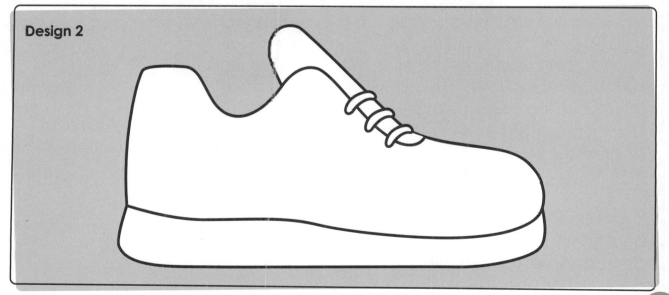

In the first design box, design a fun pair of sneakers. Use your favorite colors, images, or characters. Make the sneakers as colorful or sparkly as you like.

Show your design to a friend, and ask them to write feedback on page 91. Then redraw your design taking in any changes that might improve it.

HOT

In the first design box, design a fun pair of sneakers for a friend or family member. Find out what they like before you start. You could ask:

• What are your favorite colors?
• Do you like bright designs, neons, or pastels best?
• What would like to see on your sneakers?

Show your design to the person, and ask them to write feedback on page 91. Then redraw your design again taking in the changes your "customer" requested.

MEGA HOT

In the first design box, design a fun pair of sneakers. Use complementary colors to make the design bright and eye-catching.

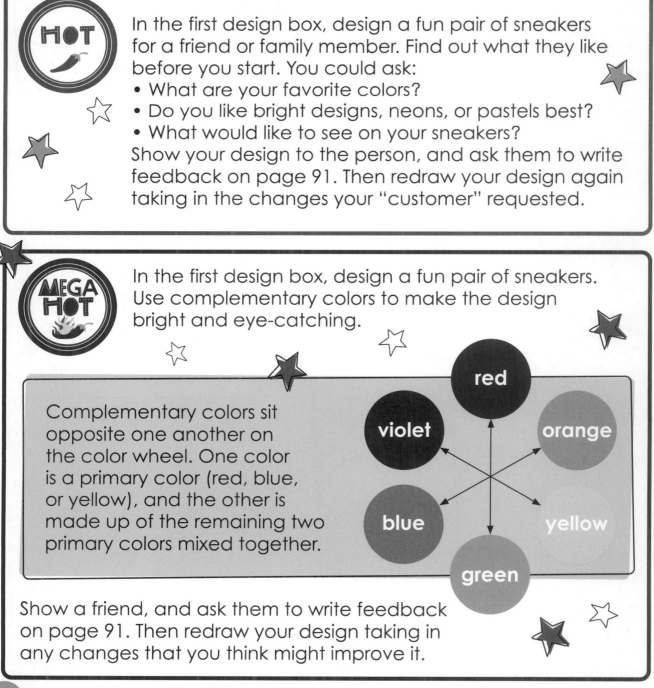

Complementary colors sit opposite one another on the color wheel. One color is a primary color (red, blue, or yellow), and the other is made up of the remaining two primary colors mixed together.

red
violet
orange
blue
yellow
green

Show a friend, and ask them to write feedback on page 91. Then redraw your design taking in any changes that you think might improve it.

Snazzy Sneakers Evaluation

Challenge Level

Date: ....

Ask someone to give you feedback on your work.

Things that look good:

_____

_____

Things that could be improved:

_____

_____

Try again, using the feedback. Then answer the questions below.

How did you feel when you received feedback? _____

_____

Was your second attempt better than your first? Why? _____

_____

What have you learned from this challenge? _____

_____

Fruit and Vegetable Art

If you stop trying to prove that you're clever or talented, you'll be able to relax and enjoy the learning process.

Fruits and vegetables come in lots of different shapes, sizes, and colors. They are perfect for making art you can eat. Choose the challenge that's right for you.

SPICY

Create characters out of these fruit and vegetables. Give each character a different personality. You could add eyes, ears, glasses, hats, mustaches, hair, and jewelry. Give each character a name, such as Brenda Broccoli or Bertie Banana.

Have fun creating a 3D animal out of fruit and vegetables. You could use toothpicks to join the pieces. If you use a knife, make sure an adult is supervising you. When you're happy with your creation, take a photo to remember it. Then eat and enjoy!

In the 1500s, Italian artist Giuseppe Arcimboldo painted some unusual portraits. His faces were made of fruits, vegetables, and flowers. What different foods can you find in this painting?

Now, either draw or paint a face using only fruits, vegetables, and flowers as Arcimboldo did, or make a face from pieces of fruits and vegetables.

Fruit and Vegetable Art Evaluation

Challenge Level

Date: ....

Did you choose the right challenge level for you?

Where are you on your learning journey?

What did you do well? ______

What did you find difficult? ______

What can't you do YET? ______

What have you learned from this challenge? ______

Did you think about giving up? What made you keep going? ______

If you failed, will you try again? Why? ______

REWARD CHART

Each time you complete a challenge, place a sticker in the correct box below. Choose a spicy, hot, or mega-hot sticker to record the level you've achieved so far.

Challenges

STORY MAKER
PAGE 7

THE SECRET DOOR
PAGE 10

HOMOPHONES
PAGE 13

A SPECIAL GIFT
PAGE 16

WEIRD AND WONDERFUL WORDS
PAGE 18

GAME ON!
PAGE 21

VACATION ISLAND
PAGE 25

LAVA LAMP
PAGE 29

BALLOON POWER
PAGE 32

ODDS AND EVENS
PAGE 36

SECRET MESSAGES
PAGE 39

RACE CAR RAMPS
PAGE 41

BEAN JOURNAL
PAGE 44

MONEY SPIDERS
PAGE 48

FIVE-DAY FITNESS CHALLENGE
PAGE 51

SUPER-FIT SUPERHERO
PAGE 53

SOCCER-BALL JUGGLING
PAGE 56

PICK-UP CHALLENGE
PAGE 59

THAT'S MAGIC!
PAGE 62

BUCKET BALL
PAGE 65

BALLOON TENNIS
PAGE 68

RIBBON DANCING
PAGE 70

CREATE CALLIGRAMS
PAGE 73

SELF-PORTRAIT
PAGE 77

BUBBLE LETTERS
PAGE 80

SHAPE PICTURES
PAGE 83

POINTILLISM
PAGE 86

SNAZZY SNEAKERS
PAGE 89

FRUIT AND VEGETABLE ART
PAGE 92

CONGRATULATIONS!

HARD WORK AWARD!

Name: ....

has successfully completed the

BiG BOOK OF ACTIVITIES FOR KiDS

Date: ....

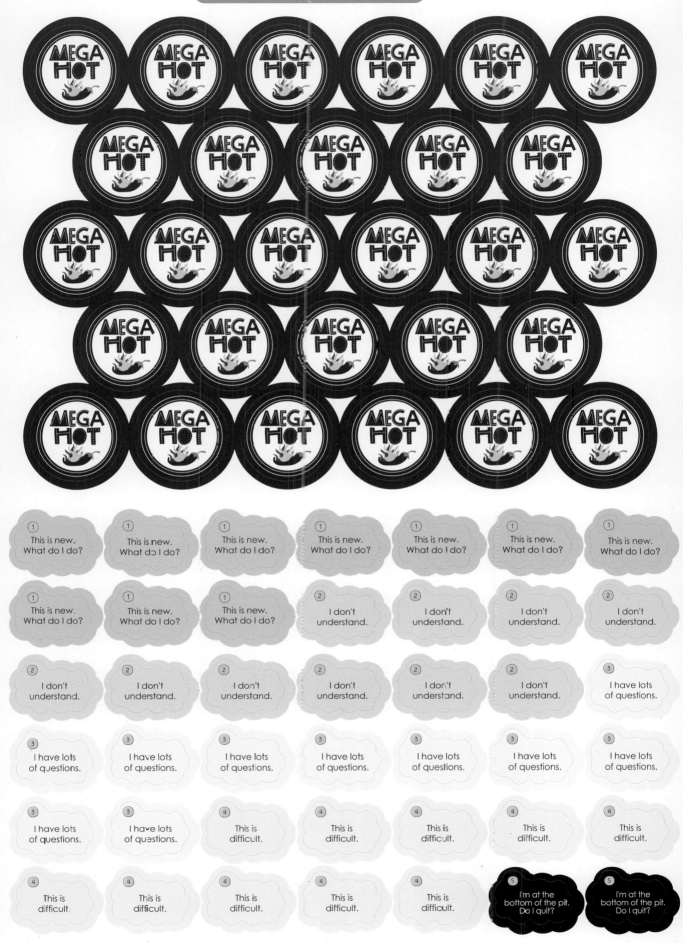

EVALUATION STICKERS

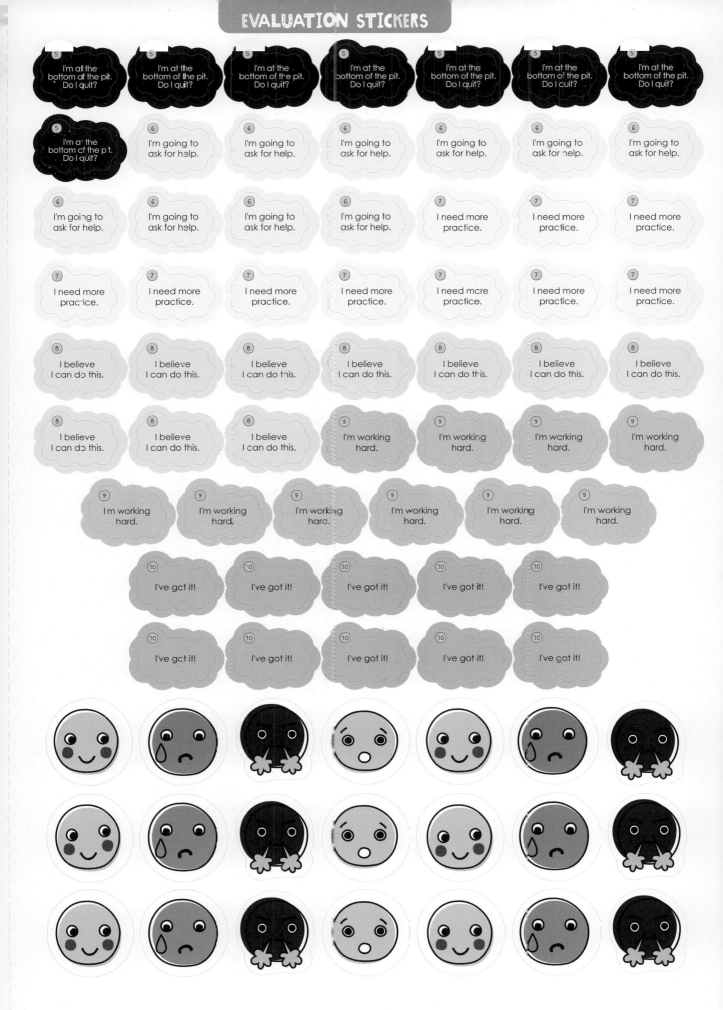

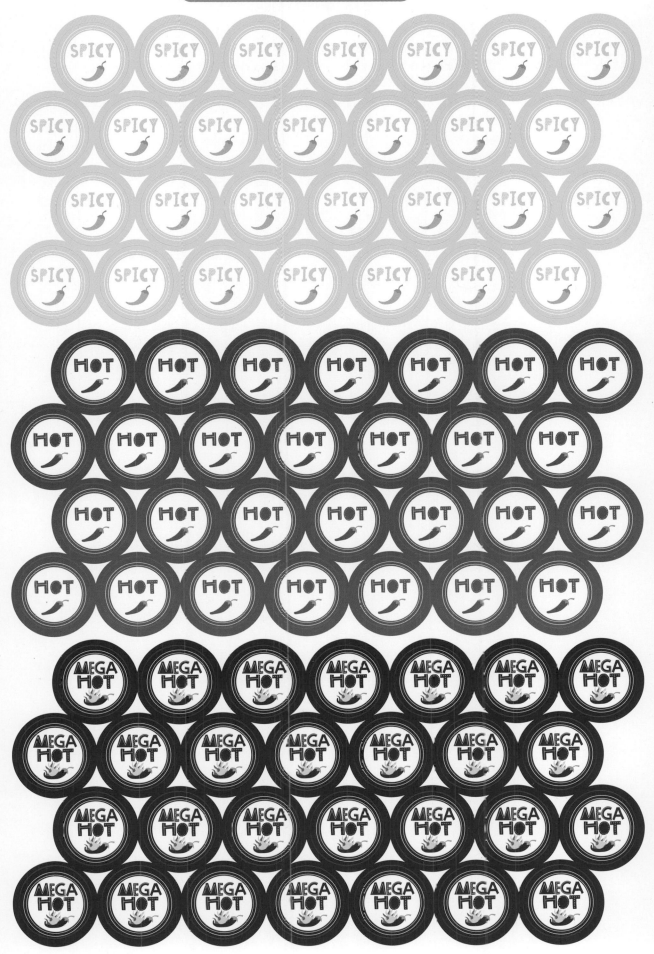